HOUSE OF
CASH

HOUSE OF CASH

THE LEGACIES OF MY FATHER, JOHNNY CASH

JOHN CARTER CASH

INSIGHT 👁 EDITIONS

San Rafael, California

CONTENTS

CHAPTER ONE

FRUITS OF THE SPIRIT

Dad literally carried me around the world with him through the early years of my life.

My father was a complicated man. There is no denying that. He was a man of steadfast faith and an open book in so many ways. But he was also a very deep and even mysterious man, intriguing and unpredictable. Some may have argued that he was defined by his failures, struggles, addictions, and pains. Kris Kristofferson called Dad "a walking contradiction, partly truth and partly fiction." He could not have been more aptly described. But the things that made him great were not these contradictions.

I feel it is important to share facets of my father's nature that are unknown to many of his fans. He was in many ways a simple man, giving and loving. He was brought up by a devout but non-judgmental Christian family, the very salt of the American earth. He was creative throughout his life and not only with music. He was a poet, painter, photographer, humorist, cook, and fisherman—to list only a few of his talents.

I see my father through the world's eyes quite often, and to me there is much missing in the common perception of the man. To some he is the ultimate image of cool. His tough, haggard image is alluring and intriguing, and punks and rockers around the world appreciate him as much as country music fans. However, beneath the surface there is much more. This book offers a deeper understanding of who Johnny Cash really was, beyond the illusion.

At the same time, there is really no way I could completely explain my father. I do not comprehend him fully myself and don't believe anyone alive does. Within these pages may be found a better understanding, but not a definitive solution to the mystery of exactly who he was. While so much is easily understood, the deeper one looks into Dad's life, the more perplexed one may become. With his songs he mesmerizes us, and with his dark and seemingly magical eyes he confuses us. But I feel this happens only when we lose sight of the simple defining characteristics that made up the man.

Neither of my parents ever threw anything away. They gave things away all the time, amazing gifts on occasion, often on a whim to a loved one—beautiful guitars, suits of clothes, automobiles, all sorts of things. But throw anything away? Never. They had a storage vault in their office that they continually added to through the years, until it was full to capacity by the ends of their lives. After my parents passed, it became our job to go through these items and catalog them. I must give thanks to my wife, Laura, for her dedication to this daunting task, and to all who helped along the way.

There were master tapes dating from the mid-1950s through the early 2000s; there were also guns, clothes, railroad spikes, film reels, saddles (both for horse and camel), sketches, paintings, dried flowers, folders of song lyrics, bags filled with cassette tapes, stack after stack of quarter-inch audio tape mixes, strange hats, guitar cases (both empty and containing guitars), harmonicas, various piles of blank stationery, microphones, press promotion photos, phonograph records and players, and innumerable family, personal, stage, and random photographs. This list could go on and on.

Among the items we combed through were some treasures of great personal value. The songs, poetry, and other writings; the images; and the artifacts offered a clearer view of who my father really was. It became my mission to share what I felt he would have liked people to know about him. That is the essence of this book.

I have never forgotten one night late in the fall of 1974, in Davenport, Iowa. I was four years old. Dad stood beside me onstage, holding my hand and larger than life. My hair was red, unlike his, although my eyes were the same deep brown. I wanted to have black hair back then, wanted to be like him in every way. I could smell the alligator leather boots he wore. They were almost as tall as me, laced up to the knee and glowing with the sheen of many fevered rubbings. Dad loved his black shoe polish. He'd developed the habit of polishing his own boots during his time in the air force and continued it his whole life. He kept shoe polish in almost every drawer in his closet, in the cabinet beside his bed, and in his toiletries bag.

Onstage I could almost see my reflection in those boots. I was wearing my stage overalls, hand-embroidered with rainbows and a farm scene by my mother. She was onstage also, and we were singing "Can the Circle Be Unbroken." It was a song from her family—the Carter Family—and we sang it on every show. I bellowed loudly into my microphone. My pitch was bad back then. I could hear the melody, but without formal training, staying in tune was something else. Still, I sang with every bit of energy I had.

From the moment I could walk, my parents brought me onstage. They stood me in between them, gave me the mic, and told me to sing along. That night when the song ended, Dad turned to me.

"Thanks to John Carter for helping us with that one!"

The crowd roared. I felt the familiar bloom of joy inside. I loved the applause. It was addictive.

"Where are you going now, John Carter?" the man at my side asked, the entertainer, my father, and my idol.

"I'm going fishing," I answered.

"You got worms?"

"Yep, but I'm going anyway."

The crowd burst into laughter. My one joke. It was always a hit.

Dad turned to the bandleader, Bob Wootton. "Bob, kick off 'Daddy Sang Bas—'"

"I've got a song I want to sing," I said loudly into the microphone. Bob looked at me questioningly. Dad turned to me, uncertainty in his eyes.

"Well, all right then," he said, after just the shortest of pauses. I chanced a glance at my mother; she was smiling, but had the same uncertain nervousness in her gaze.

I turned to the expectant crowd and sang, "I keep my pants up with a piece of twine, I keep my eyes wide open, I keep the ends out for the ties that bind, because you're mine." At that point I paused for effect, looking around. All eyes were on me. "I pull the twine!" I finished. The crowd did not disappoint me with their response.

Bob hit the first lick of "Daddy Sang Bass" on his guitar, but I called out loudly, "Wait! Wait! I've got another song!" My father turned to me with an unfamiliar stern gaze. I paid no heed. I glanced at my mother. She also eyed me incredulously. Bob stopped playing, looking to my father for direction.

The crowd had grown quiet. I had their attention.

"I'm being swallowed by a boa constrictor, a boa constrictor, a boa constrictor. I'm being swallowed by a boa constrictor, and I go down, down, down . . . Oh no." I looked at my father for support. He responded with a half smile. "There goes my toe. Oh, me—there goes my knee. Oh, fiddle," I wrapped my arms around my waist, tightening them, "It's up to my middle. Oh heck—it's up to my neck!" my hands around my neck. "Oh, dread—it's up to my . . . " at this I broke off into a garble of unintelligible sounds. The crowd once again laughed, but this time not with the same enthusiasm as before.

"That was wonderful, son," my mother said this time. "Now here we go! 'Daddy Sang Bass'!"

Bob again kicked off the song. "Wait! Wait!" I cried. "I've got another song!" My father looked at me sternly. It was that same look I was unfamiliar with. His frown froze my words in my throat. My mother walked over to me and put her arm around me. My father, looming over me like a great oak tree, put his great hand on top of my little head, applying gentle but steady pressure. This time, Bob did not stop.

After the song, I headed to the dressing room with Mom. "Wait here for your father," she said. "I know he will want to talk to you. You were a bit out of hand onstage tonight, son."

"I was just wanting to sing a song, Momma."

"Well, there is a time for that, and you had your song. You were trying for too much. Now you just sit here and wait. Your dad will come see you after his encore."

So I sat and waited, anticipating what was to come. Waiting was the worst part of all. I listened first to the hypnotic drone of "I Walk the Line" and then the thunderous rumble of "Orange Blossom Special," Dad's harmonica wailing through it.

After the song ended, the applause died as the house lights came on. I heard the steady beat of those giant boots pounding down the hall, step by great step, toward the dressing room. I'd never feared my father, but I knew that I was in trouble then, and with each step, my heart beat harder until it was pounding in my ears in time with the thumping of those boots. The footfalls stopped outside the dressing room door.

Then the door handle turned, and slowly the door opened. There stood my father, looking huge. I cowered. He walked through the door and over to me. Then he kneeled on one knee, the sweat from the three-hour performance thick on his face and dampening his clothes. He moved close to me, his nose almost touching mine. We were eye to eye.

"Never. Never do that again," he said quietly and without anger. Then he smiled.

Dad let anger and frustration drift away from him with effortless calm. He never remained angry with me, never raised his voice to me except on rare occasions, and it was usually only to get my attention and keep me from hurting myself.

When I was growing up, we spent a great deal of time in New York City. My parents had an apartment at 40 Central Park South, a penthouse overlooking the park. One day we were leaving the apartment, bound for Greenwich Village and Dad's favorite guitar shop. We climbed in our normal hire, a burgundy stretch limousine. As we weaved through traffic along the park toward Fifth Avenue, there came a sudden and unexpected crash. An entire window burst into a thousand pieces. Tiny shards of glass exploded everywhere, covering my mother and myself. Though we were all in shock, my mother sat still and did not scream.

"Is everyone alright?" called the driver from the front.

"I'm okay," answered my mother.

The car came to an immediate halt, and I saw my father reach and grab something from the floorboard—a sizable rock. He burst from the door and rushed to the sidewalk.

I moved toward the open door to follow, but my mother stopped me. "Stay still, son," she commanded as calmly as possible. The broken glass was all over her, though she did not seem to be hurt or bleeding at all.

A tall, shirtless young man was standing on the sidewalk, his eyes glazed over and his face blank. My father's face reddened with anger and he rushed up to him.

"Is this your rock?" he demanded.

The man began to jabber in a language I did not understand. There were a few English words mixed in, but not many.

I saw my father stand there, staring into the stranger's eyes. For a brief moment, I wondered if Dad was going to hit him, perhaps with the same rock the man had thrown through our window. But Dad only stood there, eye to eye with the tall foreigner. Then Dad held out the rock again. "Take it," he said.

The man stopped talking and reached out his hand and took the rock.

"Go put this back where you found it, please," said my father, and then turned his back and walked to the car.

By this time, my mother and I had brushed off most of the glass. Except for a few tiny nicks, we were untouched.

"Good Lord, John. I am uncut. It is a miracle. What on earth was wrong with that young man?" My mother's grace was evident from her calm tone.

"I think he was on drugs, June," answered my dad. "I don't even think he knew where he was, much less that he threw a rock at somebody's big red limo."

I looked out the window and saw the man sitting on the curbside, staring down at the rock in his hand as if it had magically appeared there.

"Let's pray for him," said my father. "Stay in the car, son."

And so my mother and father got out of the car and walked over to the man. He looked up, not seeming to recognize my father as the same person who had just handed him the rock. I saw my father bend down on one knee, and then my mother with him. As they prayed, the man closed his eyes and began to cry.

Now when I think back and remember that day, I find a great lesson. My father showed that man immediate forgiveness and tenderness. There was never a moment's hesitation on Dad's part once he realized the man was confused and in pain. My mother was right beside him.

My father was a gentle man.

True love is many things and can survive the strongest and most painful of times. When love comes out the other side of a fire, it may be scarred forever, but this bruised love is somehow only greater for having survived the pain. This was the kind of love my father and mother shared, a love that survived the greatest of struggles, sank to the depths of misery, and still came out the other side stronger than before. How was this possible? Shortly before he died, my father told me that it was the ability of the soul to forgive that kept love strong. He said that through it all, if we are able to forgive and forget the pain caused by the ones we love, we will find that our love has grown. He didn't have to tell me this, though; I saw it by his and my mother's examples.

Valentine's Day 1987 was cold. My parents had not worked much that year and we were at home that day. It was late morning, and my mother and I were in the kitchen eating one of my mother's favorite breakfasts: tomato gravy and homemade biscuits. Mom slopped a second helping of this milky-pink concoction on my biscuits and I dug in. We had not seen Dad yet that morning.

I was beginning to wonder if he was going to sleep until noon, when I heard his footsteps descending the stairs, his stockinged feet gently padding along carefully. It had not been long since he'd had surgery on his knee, and he moved cautiously. He walked into the kitchen, an item in each arm. One was a small package, wrapped in shiny red paper and tied with bright crimson ribbon. The other was a folded piece of light-blue paper, my mother's favorite color.

Mom turned to him and smiled. "Happy Valentine's Day," he said, and handed her the card. She opened it and gazed upon the inscription within. I leaned over between bites and took a quick look. It was a simple design, just a statement of his love for her, but her eyes lit up with a blaze.

"Oh, honey, I love you," she said, and he bent and hugged her.

Then he handed her the package. She flipped open the top of the box and inside found a ring with a shiny stone, deep red and so bright it almost hurt my eyes.

"That's beautiful, John," she said, and slid the ring on her finger. She put on her glasses and stared into its ruby depths. Then she did the most curious thing: She took off the ring and put it back in its box, sat it down beside her plate, and picked up the card again. She opened it and once again read the words. I noticed the light in her eyes was much brighter when she looked at the card than when she focused on the ring.

The greater gift was the handmade card. And he gave her one every year. Even though the cards were often accompanied by a diamond necklace or some other piece of precious jewelry, it was the creative work that she was most touched by.

He never stopped writing to her, sending her love notes and letters. She cleared his spirit so many times of the dust and darkness, the anger and pain that often engulfed his life. He knew inside—though at times he obviously forgot—that she was more than he deserved, that she was his only by some grace God had provided him. And when he did forget, it was only temporary, and he would always remember again. And he would write to her.

Dad adored my mother. He cherished her as his greatest jewel, the way a shallower man would have cherished great riches. Dad would have cast all else aside at any time to keep my mother.

When my mother died on May 15, 2003, my father began to sell or give away all his possessions. Without her, nothing physical held any value to him anymore. His greatest treasure was gone.

My dad identified with the Old Testament character Job, who lost all. Dad was also familiar with suffering. He had chronic problems with his knee, beginning in the 1970s after he fell in an open boat well. He had three ribs broken once when a pet ostrich kicked him while attempting to disembowel him. After Dad broke his jaw in 1990, he had a bone graft, but the nerve did not heal right.

It left him in chronic pain for the last thirteen years of his life. I believe Dad, like Job, never cursed God, but rather came to accept his burden as best as a human could.

Dad "owned his pain," as he told me once. He was continuously hungry for spiritual wisdom, and the one subject on which he focused more than any other was the Bible. When his pains—both physical and psychological—bore down on him, he went deeper into his study of the Scriptures. He was always looking for a better understanding of life and the troubles that came along with it. Whether they were struggles in his career or broken bones, Dad used these obstacles as stepping-stones to a greater spiritual understanding, a means of becoming closer to God. He once wrote, "The Master of Life's been good to me. He has given me strength to face past illnesses, and victory in the face of defeat. He has given me life and joy where others saw oblivion. He has given me a new purpose to live for, new services to render, and old wounds to heal."

When Dad suffered, he turned to music as well as to the Bible. Despite his setbacks, he never ceased working. In 1993 he began what I will argue was his most impressive and significant body of work, the records he made with producer Rick Rubin. Why his most significant work? Throughout his later years, his physical ailments were unending, but he never gave up. The pain was always there. His respiratory sicknesses came and went. He was in and out of the hospital all the time. He suffered from a neuropathic condition akin to Parkinson's disease, which the doctors initially diagnosed as a rare condition called Shy-Drager Syndrome. Later this diagnosis was discounted and it was determined he suffered from a condition known as autonomic neuropathy. Still, he never gave up. He continued making music and writing.

Dad retired from the road in 1997 because of this disease and intended to slow down. But he did not. It seemed that his restlessness only grew with his newfound idle time. He went back into the studio again and again. One week he would be in the hospital fighting another battle with pneumonia; two weeks later he would be finishing up what would become another Grammy-winning CD. From the time he retired until the last week of his life, he worked on his music. Without a doubt, his greatest suffering came after my mother died. But even then he did not stop, instead redoubled his efforts.

I remember clearly, though through the haze of grief, the day of my mother's funeral. It was one of the longest days in my life, and most assuredly the longest in my father's. We left the grave site that day in a long stretch limo, my father and I along with my sisters. When we were barely out of the cemetery, Dad turned to me.

"I am ready to go in the studio, son," he said with haggard conviction. "I need to," he said.

"Are you sure, Dad?" I asked. My sisters heard him say this and looked on in surprise. "Are you sure you don't want to wait a week or so?"

"See if you can set up a session in three days," he said with tired determination.

And so in three days' time we were in the studio. The music was his therapy, his solace. But it was so much more to him. In the music he found strength and purpose, and through the music he grieved more truly. Behind his final musical works was an almost preternatural persistence. His eyes were blind, his body was failing, but he pressed on.

It is one thing to make a great body of work while you're strong and in your prime. It is another to create such a body of work while battling suffering and sickness, continuing on through these storms with the determination of a captain at the helm of a great ship in a hurricane.

Dad's spirit did not give up. His body lost its ability to carry on, but if he had been able to, he would still be making music today. I have been asked if my father died of a broken heart. Certainly his heart was broken when he passed. But this did not kill him. His fortitude was inviolable, though his body would not last.

In sum, if I were asked to say exactly who my father was, I would answer that he was a gentle, loving, and persistent man. Oh, yes, there is so much more to who he was. Many knew him to challenge authority, and he was famous for his devil-may-care attitude. His compassion for the down-and-out marked his music, which has touched the lives of many people, without a doubt. All around the globe and in all walks of life, one can find his fans. An elderly farmer from Topeka, Kansas, is just as likely to have a comprehensive collection of Dad's music as a punk rock fan from Hamburg, Germany. His influence is far-reaching, to say the least. But Johnny Cash had the most profound hold on the hearts of those who were closest to him.

How can it be demonstrated that he was gentler than he was angry, more kind than forceful, more meek than boastful, and more loving than spiteful? How can I express the affection and support he gave to his loved ones, the faith he shared, and the spirit of giving he possessed?

How will Johnny Cash be remembered? As a face on a web page, an image across a screen, and only the memory of his voice from a digital file or the rust of tape? As the resounding tones of a baritone voice or the defining sound of his boom-chicka-boom across the acoustic strings of his Martin D-28? Will he be remembered by a music video where he digs back through a painful past and reflects in pain the sufferings and hurts he lived and caused? Are all these true pictures of the man? Yes, in part. Most certainly.

But my father was so much more.

So let me share what memories and insight I have into who the man was beyond the song, and what the contours were of the spiritual and creative world in which he lived. As you turn these pages, I hope you will discover the man I knew—the father, friend, and man of God.

CHAPTER TWO

BEGINNINGS & FOUNDATIONS

ohn R. Cash was born February 26, 1932, into a family where faith was of paramount importance. Gospel music fed his spirit and was essential to the formation of my father's Christian faith. His home was filled with gospel music. Each night the whole family would gather around the radio to hear the songs of Jimmie Davis, Sister Rosetta Tharpe, the Carter Family, and later, Hank Snow. The family's love for gospel music touched Dad's heart deeply and stayed with him his whole life.

Carrie, Dad's mother, had an old guitar and played just a little—only a few chords, really. But Dad told me the first music he ever heard came from her lips. Although life was hard in Arkansas for the Cashes, there was always music.

Dad wrote, "Babies get hungry if they aren't fed, and the babies of Ray and Carrie Cash were born into a world where times were mighty tough. But throughout the tough years of the Depression, up through the . . . thirties and forties, Ray Cash found honest work to feed his family."

In 1935 the Cashes moved from Kingsland, in southern Arkansas, to Dyess, in the northeast corner of the state. Their new town was a place of hope for farmers who had been granted land as part of Franklin Delano Roosevelt's New Deal. They all worked hard to make something of the dark earth, or gumbo, as it was called in that area.

I have often heard it said that my grandfather was a share-cropper, but that is not true. Under FDR's program, the farmers actually owned their land. In the spring the Cashes planted cotton seeds in the rich, black dirt. Come harvest, the entire family, young and old, picked the cotton all day, dawn to dusk, their fingers bleeding, their backs sore. "At times Carrie did this hard work while pregnant with another baby," my father wrote, "in order to help Ray Cash, who did every kind of labor known." And they sang through this labor, easing their souls. Most of the songs were from my grandmother's favorite southern gospel hymnal.

Very early on Dad showed great artistic potential, which can be clearly seen in his poetry and songs.

When my father was a boy, he and his brother Jack, who was two year older, were always together. Jack was Dad's best friend, and Dad looked up to him. Jack was strong and full of the love for God. He aspired at an early age to become a pastor and was on his way, studying the Bible daily.

"Jack never ceased praying," my father told me once. "His lips were continuously moving. I asked Jack what he was saying once, and he told me he was just talking to God."

In the summer of 1944, when my father was twelve years old, Jack suffered a tragic, fatal accident while working with a pendulum saw. When Jack died, my dad was visited by an angel.

I will never forget the way Dad disclosed this experience. We were traveling by bus across western Canada, en route from Banff to Vancouver. It was late summer, and the sky was almost clear. I saw wisps of clouds high above us and daydreamed about flying between them, looking for angels.

We were in Dad's private room on the bus, relaxing on the black leather couches as we barreled down the highway. "Dad, do you believe in angels?" I asked him.

"Oh, certainly, son," he replied. "I had a conversation with one once."

"Really, Daddy?" I asked. I was no more than ten.

Dad closed his eyes for a moment.

"Yes, son," he said, his eyes now focusing on mine. "After Jack's accident I couldn't sleep. So I would go out on the porch at night. When I sat down it was late afternoon, but I must have fallen asleep because all I remember was waking to the night. There was someone on the porch with me."

"Who was it, Daddy?"

"It was a man, son. Dressed in a gray suit," said Dad.

"Was it an angel, Daddy? Did he have wings?"

Dad smiled. "No, son. No wings. But I knew he was an angel." Dad picked up the Bible that always sat on the table in his private room and unconsciously leafed through the pages.

"I asked him," he said, "if he would take me instead of Jack. He said no, that it was not my time."

When I asked Dad if he had seen an angel since then, he said he didn't know for sure, but that he might have. And he continued to believe in them. I have been looking for them myself ever since that bus ride.

It took days for Jack to finally die as a result of complications from an infection. His death shattered my father, who was by Jack's side while he suffered. When Jack died, a part of my father almost certainly stopped growing in some way. Nevertheless, Dad matured a great deal through this experience, and his spirit became stronger as a result of the pain.

On the day of Jack's death, my father went to the grave site early. He joined the workers and helped dig the grave. He had stepped on a nail a few days before, and his swollen foot would not fit inside his shoe. So at Jack's burial service that day, my dad was without shoes, his clothes dirty from all the digging. My father's sister Joanne told me this story. It reflected his determination and his boundless love for his brother. Maybe this pain was the crucible that helped my dad become the man he was destined to be, a better, stronger man. Four years after Jack's death, when my father was sixteen, he wrote the following:

But when I awoke the morrow morn
I found this beggar gone.
And he left a piece of paper
With these words so true and plain
"You have carried away someone's burdens.
You have not lived life in vain."
And if it was before me,
I would do it all again
Just to help some weary pilgrim
And not live life in vain.

These early years open a window into my father's nature. He was fiercely dedicated to his family all through his life, keeping his parents close to him. I never saw Dad disrespect them. He didn't argue or talk back, at least not in front of me. He taught me, "Honor your mother and father," and Dad lived by this golden rule.

I believe there was a mutual respect, which my grandparents shared with each of their children. My grandfather was certainly a tough man, hardworking with a strong personality. I am not saying the man was a saint. I know he had a temper and liked to drink, at least early in his life. But my father said he had never seen his father hit anyone, stranger or family.

When he was growing up, my father was called JR Cash. The "R" did not stand for anything, and in discussing this with relatives, I discovered a mild controversy. My grandmother Carrie's family name was Rivers, and she wanted to name my father John Rivers Cash, while my grandfather Ray wanted to name him John Ray Cash. As a compromise, they decided to give Dad a middle initial instead of a middle name. This was quite common back then.

Dad worked the cotton fields all his years growing up; he worked hard, like the rest of the family. His life consisted of school, work in the cotton fields in the afternoon, music from the family radio in the evening, and the Saturday movie at the Dyess theater. The town of Dyess, albeit wonderful in its own way, held no future for my father.

Although Dad had many great memories of his childhood home, it is evident that he could not wait to get out. In 1950 he did just that, joining the air force and taking an extended tour to Germany. When he went to the recruiting office and produced his birth certificate, the name on it was JR Cash.

"You have to have a first name," the recruiter told Dad.

"John," my father answered, though few people had ever called him that. And so JR Cash became John R. Cash. He was a high-speed Morse code interceptor and was very good at what he did. Even later in life, he could still write and read Morse code, and proved it to me once by writing out the Twenty-Third Psalm in the staggered code of dots and dashes. I wish I had kept that piece of paper. I don't know what happened to it.

Dad was very creative during his time in Germany, and wrote an early version of what would become "Folsom Prison Blues" while he was there. He also bought his first guitar in Germany, near the base in Landsberg. Here is a comic piece that he wrote during that time:

THE FLIGHT BEFORE CHRISTMAS

'Twas the flight before Christmas, and all down below,
Not a thing was I seeing, not even the snow.
Visibility was zero, no stars were in sight.
It was promising to be a heck of a night.
The co-pilot was sleeping, but not in his bed
While visions of Broadway danced in his head.
The rest of the crew was just sitting around.

Thinking of life in the old home town.
And I, in my cockpit had set the controls
Hoping the fuel was going to hold.
When on engine "4" there arose such a clatter
I started checking the dials to see what's the matter.
And doing so, this instantly came to mind;
the R.P.M. was only half time!
With the old inter-com I yelled, "Pilot to crew!
Number 4 is kapoot! You know what to do."
I opened the throttle on old number 4
But only three engines were making her roar.
So I set up the crate so she'd run on the three.
And told the Radio Operator to get on the key.
I knew that our field must be pretty near,
If it wasn't, then we'd never see the new year.
After minutes of sweating they finally came through
And said their visibility was zero, too!
So they picked us up with their radar eyes,
And started giving us intro to fly.
"Two degrees to the left, and keep on the line.
You don't see us, but you're coming in fine.
Drop her a little now, and drop her slow
There's just about 4 more minutes to go.
Altitude 300, you're coming in Roger!
The strip's just ahead, so buddy don't dodge her."
Visibility zero, I still couldn't see.
But thank God the G.C.A. man saw me.
Then the final command, "Gear down and roll!"

I rubbed mother earth, and we'd reached our goal.
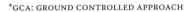
When we came to a stop, and finally unpacked
I felt like Santa Claus opening his sack.
And when I crawled in my sack at the end of the day,
I was thanking my God for G.C.A.*
And I heard the boys say, when they turned off the light,
"Merry Christmas to all, and brother what a night!"

*GCA: GROUND CONTROLLED APPROACH

When my father completed his tour of duty in 1954, he did not return to Dyess. Instead, he settled in Memphis, Tennessee, and married Vivian Liberto. He loved Vivian dearly and had written her constantly while on his tour of duty. Dad tried a variety of jobs: He was a door-to-door salesman, and he worked with his brother Roy for a while in the auto industry. But his heart kept wanting more.

Rosanne, Dad and Vivian's eldest child, was born in 1955. Three more girls, Kathy, Cindy, and Tara, followed Roseanne. Soon after Rosanne's birth, he began to work hard on his music. Dad was limited as a guitar player—and never believed otherwise. But there was something about his style that was special.

In 1954, Dad walked into Sun Records and right up to the producer, Sam Phillips. He introduced himself as John R. Cash and said he wanted to record gospel music. Dad sang a hit record for Sam by Governor Jimmie Davis, "I Was There When It Happened." Sam immediately saw the potential in my father, but he was not looking for a gospel singer. He told my dad to come back when he had some original material worked up. Dad did come back, with "Hey Porter" and "Cry, Cry, Cry." Sam signed him to Sun Records, where Carl Perkins and Elvis Presley, among others, were already on the roster.

In the 1960s Dad fell into an emotionally darker period. He struggled with a feeling of isolation, which was aggravated by the remoteness that comes with fame. Drug addiction also held a powerful control over his life. He spent countless hours in the desert alone. His home life with Vivian was in shambles and Rosanne, Kathy, Cindy, and Tara were suffering because of it.

Despite these personal difficulties, Dad forged ahead and broke new ground in music, his creative energy unabated. His concept albums *Ballads of the True West* and *Bitter Tears* were like nothing that had come before. It was after their release that the concept album took hold in popular music. Dad led the way, most certainly. Music was solace to him, just as it had been when he was a boy. He never lost his passion for it.

My father had first used drugs in the 1950s, but it was in the mid-1960s that his addiction took a deeper and deeper hold on his life. I can remember when I was young, my father saw a photo of himself taken during 1966 and said simply, "That is a very sick man."

Dad hit a hard rock bottom sometime in the fall of 1967. The pills he was on stopped helping, and he nearly died. Those who loved him, including a strong and loving woman he had adored his whole life, offered great help. Finally, he managed to pull himself through and rededicate his life to Christ.

CHAPTER THREE

FAITH

& PHILOSOPHY

The man I remember from my early childhood was strong and certain, consistent and trustworthy. He was widely famous by that time, a household name, really. He and my mom spent much of their time traveling the world, and they took me with them. We traveled to Europe, Australia, Asia, and Africa. By the time I was nine, I had been to more than thirty countries, including the Holy Land and almost all fifty states, always by my parents' sides.

Dad had a great love for the Holy Land. I was but a baby on my first trip there, when he was making the film that he produced on the life of Christ, *Gospel Road*. Numerous trips to the Holy Land followed.

In 1977 Mom and Dad took a large group of people with them to Israel. They loved the people they employed, and they showed it by selling their Rolls-Royce limousine and spending every penny from the sale on a two-week tour through the Holy Land for each and every employee, and most of the family—over thirty people. I will never forget that trip; we all grew closer together because of it. As for my parents, their relationship remained strong, their love true and clear.

My dad valued education—he was a lifelong student himself. So when I was six, he and my mom decided I should stay home so I could go to school during the fall and spring, when they toured. They employed Winifred and George Kelly to watch over me. These deeply spiritual people were kind and strong Seventh-Day Adventists. They cared for me with deep devotion. For our family, home life was good and road life was an adventure. Dad was clear-eyed and spiritual, and it seemed as if his addiction was a thing of the past. This was the life I knew then.

The one thing that was constant in my father's life was his religious conviction. He remained a Christian man of faith, and from this he never strayed, eventually becoming an ordained minister. He was always willing to offer his testimony. Although the weight of stardom sometimes settled heavily on his shoulders, he would step up to the pulpit for this purpose any time. He believed it his duty as a Christian to share his salvation.

Dad was not a judgmental type of Christian. He was open to people from all religious denominations. My father focused on the Bible as the source of his own Christian faith and did not lean so much on the offerings of any denomination in particular.

Though Dad grew up Southern Baptist, he went to the churches of a variety of denominations through his life. In the 1960s Rev. Floyd Gressett of the Avenue Community Church in Ventura helped Dad find recovery and reaffirm his salvation. In the early 1970s my parents were members of Rev. Jimmie Snow's Evangel Temple in Madison. They would bring the whole family to worship there, including my sisters, whenever they were in from California. My mother's daughters, Rozanna and Carlene, came, too, as did good friends, such as Kris Kristofferson and Larry Gatlin. Jimmie's preaching was full of the spirit, and Dad and Mom were forever eager to sing along to the music. But eventually, we left the Evangel Temple and became members at the Hendersonville Church of God, pastored by John Colbaugh.

Pastor Colbaugh was a dear friend to my dad, and it was at this church that I found my own salvation and was baptized at the age of nine. Dad was beside me that day and was thrilled. He often said, "I have no greater joy than to see my children walk in the truth." Another Christian brother and spiritual counselor was Rev. Jack Shaw, who traveled as part of our touring group in the mid- to late 1990s, through the last few years of the road show, up until my father disbanded it in 1997. Jack was a gentle and wise man with a unique vision: to open a hospital in Nakuru, Kenya. Dad supported these endeavors, and the family still supports Jack's ministry today. Dad also gave his friend and advisor Nat Winston a lot of credit for his spiritual influence.

Dad had many who helped him along his spiritual path, true friends who did not want anything from him but to be his friend and support him when needed. These spiritual advisors were just a few of those who shaped his life. There were too many to mention them all, but undeniably one of my father's dearest brothers in faith was Dr. Billy Graham. Their friendship began in the 1960s, when Dr. Graham sent a message to my father. Billy later admitted that he reached out to Dad at first in order to impress his music-loving son Franklin!

"Johnny Cash called me on the phone," Billy told me. "I was amazed. He asked me if my wife and I would come spend the night with them. I said I'd be honored."

And so Billy and Ruth Graham flew to Nashville and spent a few days with my parents. They ate good food, laughed, and got acquainted. This trip began a friendship that would last a lifetime. Over the years, Billy and Ruth and my parents spent a great deal of time fishing, swimming, relaxing—just being together. Dad and Billy studied the Bible together.

Dad was impressed by Billy's wisdom, but Billy was humble. As a boy I thought of him as a dear uncle. He was my fishing partner, too, and even helped me learn how to swim.

Dad took part in Billy's crusades year after year. He not only professed his faith with each appearance, but also spread his love for gospel music even more. He performed old standards along with songs of his own composition.

Dad stayed friends with Billy through the years. There wasn't an instance when Billy wasn't there to support him, especially through the bad times and even when he was in the throes of addiction. Just as Dad was nonjudgmental, so was Billy. They were a pair of great men, for sure. God had gifted both of them with talent and wisdom. But beneath all the trappings of their fame were the simple hearts of good men. I had always been aware of this truth, but I sensed that perhaps there was something more, something I did not understand about the men and their friendship. A few years after my father died, I set out to understand this better.

On a cold January day in 2008, I visited Billy at his home in Montreat, North Carolina. We ate ribs and talked about his relationship with my father. I felt there must have been some great mystery to such a profound and influential friendship. Look at all the people they touched through the years. Billy performed the work of God, miraculous work, as far as I was concerned. And Dad had joined him in this endeavor.

"What was the nature of your deep connection with my father?" I asked him. "What made you connect?"

"We were Christian brothers," he responded simply.

"What did you first think of my dad when you met him?"

"My first initial impression of your father was surprise," he answered. "I did not expect him to be that ordinary. I loved your father. He was one of the few men who I have really loved."

And so we finished our dinner and talked about my father and my mother, about their time together. I began to understand that the secret to their great friendship was a resounding and simple truth: Both men were seeking to grow closer to God. They both had a great love for the Bible. There was no secret of a mysterious brotherhood, just faith.

When I drove home from Billy's that day, my belly was full, and my heart was overflowing with peace and understanding.

For years, my mother and father performed as a part of Billy Graham's crusades, spreading their testimony to millions of people around the world. As Billy was my father's dear friend, Ruth Graham (beside my mother in the photo above) meant the world to my mother.

When it came to his faith, my dad used his celebrity as a platform to spread the word of Christ—and not just during Billy Graham's crusades. Dad never performed a show without singing gospel songs such as "Why Me Lord?" and "Peace in the Valley." Whether he was in the White House singing for a president or performing before hundreds of inmates at San Quentin, he never skipped the spiritual portion of the show. He got people's attention with songs like "Cocaine Blues" or "Folsom Prison Blues," his demeanor cool and dark. Then he professed his faith and sang of God and salvation. My father knew that along with all the great blessings he had been given came a great responsibility. So he used his fame to God's advantage by giving testimony.

Sometimes Dad's fame and lack of anonymity did get to him. He could not walk into a grocery store unnoticed. Once, while attending a public event in North Carolina, he tried a disguise of an orange wig and glasses. Everyone recognized him. He said later, "I didn't look like someone else. I looked like Johnny Cash in an orange wig and glasses."

I never saw my father be ungracious to his fans, despite the fact that he missed his privacy. People still come up to me and tell me of their interaction with my father and mother, how kind my parents were, and how they took the time to chat. Dad and Mom were always willing to hear fans' stories of their love for their music, no matter how trivial.

Dad had a great love for mankind in general. He not only felt this love but also showed it openly in numerous ways. When we were in New York City in 1980, the year I turned ten, I remember the cold wind blowing up and down Fifth Avenue. My mother was dressed in one of her knee-length mink coats with a matching hat. Dad was wearing a Western-style duster and no hat. We passed a man in scruffy clothes with a long, unkempt beard, who had passed out on the street. He smelled bad and I walked on past, but Dad stopped right beside the man. My mother, who was walking ahead with me, stopped also. Dad reached down and gave the man, who was regaining consciousness, a bill—a twenty. The man rolled over and a book fell from where it had been cradled against his chest as he slept. It was a Bible. The man looked up at my father. "Thanks a lot," he said groggily. He looked at my father again with a start. "Man, you look just like Johnny Cash!"

"I get that all the time," said my father, smiling.

We walked away and I heard the man call back, "Thank you again, man!" I turned to look back and saw that there was another bill I had not noticed beneath the twenty. The face of Benjamin Franklin was evident on the crisp green note—a one hundred dollar bill.

Dad raised his hand in a casual salute.

Dad never failed to take whatever time was needed to reach out to those in need, keeping his heart forever open to those who loved him. He truly cared about people. He never visited the sick or ailing for appearances, but because he felt that a great responsibility came along with fame and celebrity.

My father had a great love for biblical history and theology. In 1977 he studied with an organization called Christian International and obtained an associate's degree in biblical studies. His notes were focused and thorough, and always annotated. Dad was dedicated to reading and studying, and throughout his life he read daily. His library was full of books, including one by Josephus, the ancient Jewish historian; *The History of the Decline and Fall of the Roman Empire*, by the English historian Edward Gibbon; and many others.

Dad's love of books was shared by my mother's father, Ezra. They developed a deep friendship in the 1960s, even before he fell in love with my mother. They corresponded regularly, keeping up with each other's studies and trading tidbits of knowledge. If my mother was my father's greatest love, his second was books.

When I look at my father's and grandfather's books now, I feel as if these bound volumes themselves hold power, and perhaps they do. With all the hours these two men spent toiling over them, making notes in the margins and wearing down the bindings, perhaps some of their spirits dwell within the pages, comfortably resting on the shelves of my library. Perhaps they sleep here, awaiting the Second Coming these two men so firmly believed in.

Dad had an insatiable hunger for new knowledge, continuously delving deeper into his studies. Through all stages of his life, even throughout his addiction, he kept reading and searching. In the 1980s, after a bout with pain-pill addiction, he decided to take on the daunting task of writing a novel about the conversion of the Apostle Paul. This book, *Man in White*, which was published in 1986, is a testament to my father's love of the Scriptures. He felt a kinship with the Apostle Paul, having been blind and misled for so long and eventually finding salvation. Although Dad's career was arguably at a low point during the mid-1980s, his drug addiction prompted him to search more persistently for his salvation.

CHAPTER FOUR

MARRIED IN A
FEVER

"If you were in the country on a windless night and stood by a barbwire fence, you could hear the radio," said my father. "That was how strong the signal was from the Texas border stations."

In the late 1930s and early 1940s, a doctor named Brinkley set up an unbelievably powerful radio station, 500,000 watts, just over the border in Mexico. This was a massive signal, even by current standards, and was way over the allowed legal limit in the United States. It was from this "stage" that the world first heard the original Carter Family: A.P.; his wife Sara; his sister-in-law, Maybelle; and many more from the next generation, including Maybelle's daughters, Helen, Anita, and the energetic, rambunctious June. Literally, the entire United States heard these broadcasts. It was said that *The Carter Family Hour* was easily heard on radios as close as Memphis and as far away as Chicago and Los Angeles. It was on this radio show that a young JR Cash first heard June Carter sing and tell a few jokes.

After the first night he heard her on the radio, Dad told me, "I laughed at her all the following day long. I was enthralled with her from the moment I first heard her speak."

Dad told me something else that I never forgot: "You know how when you hear someone's voice on the radio, you get a visual idea of what they look like? And when you see the person, they never look like you pictured them? Well, it wasn't that way with your mom, son." Dad smiled. "I had never seen a picture of June when I heard her on the radio, but when I did see a picture not long after, she looked exactly like I had pictured her, just exactly."

And so JR Cash sat and listened to June and her famous family on the radio, sang her songs along with her, and dreamed.

According to legend, when my father first met June backstage at the Grand Ole Opry in 1956, he was assertive and self-assured. "Hello, I'm Johnny Cash," he had said. "I'm gonna marry you someday."

Supposedly, my mother replied sarcastically, "I can't wait." She had just divorced Carl Smith, but my father was most certainly still happily married. Their brief encounter did begin a friendship, though.

My mother had one daughter, Carlene, with Smith. The year after their divorce, she married Rip Nix. They had a daughter, Rozanna, or Rosie as we called her. My mother and Rip became separated not long after their marriage, but they did not legally divorce until 1965.

In 1962 my father asked the lady who was one day to be my mother if she would go on the road with him and open the show with her music and comedy routine. Before there were any real sparks of love, there were definitely sparks onstage. When they performed together, Mom and Dad were magical. In 1964 they recorded their first duet, "It Ain't Me, Babe," a song by my father's favorite poet, Bob Dylan.

Dad was ceaselessly searching, forever yearning for something that he felt was missing. He was assuredly in love with my mother quite a bit earlier than he was willing to admit. They were both searching, really, and Dad saw the light of home and hope in my mother.

Their relationship, onstage and off, never ceased to be a roller-coaster ride. By the mid- to late 1960s, Dad's drug addiction was in full force. His drug of choice at the time was speed (amphetamines), though he took barbiturates, too. His isolation was a huge part of his sickness back then. He would disappear, sometimes for weeks, taking his RV into the desert to try and "find himself," as he liked to put it.

My mother and Marshall Grant, Dad's longtime bass player and road manager, struggled intensely with my father at the time, as did many others. Sometimes he was hard to deal with and unpredictable. Dad and his band were all very crazy on the road. They tore out walls in hotel rooms to make connecting rooms, shot out neon signs with their pistols, and more than once released hundreds of baby chickens into a fancy hotel lobby before fleeing. They really wrote the book on the rock-star life. But neither the drummer, W. S. "Fluke" Holland, nor Marshall ever drank or did drugs. As for the wise and quiet guitarist, Luther Perkins, he was often the brunt of jokes and mostly kept to himself.

My mother supported my father and was a great friend. Dad likewise appreciated her and her whole family. He brought her sisters Anita and Helen on the road with his show, and not long after, the legendary Mother Maybelle Carter joined them.

Maybelle had never stopped playing music after the disband-
ing of the original Carter Family. She had continued to work
with her daughters, playing at the Grand Ole Opry for years and
spreading her family's music throughout the world. Now, on the
road with Johnny Cash, the Carter legacy only grew stronger.
And in this great country music family, my father saw his future,
his home.

I believe Dad carried a great deal of pain inside—pain and feelings of guilt about his rebellious lifestyle. And I think that was
largely why his addiction held such a strong grip on the man. But
along with the pain and guilt, there was faith. And in time, that
faith would prove to be the strongest force.

But before there was any redemption and change for my
father, he always had to reach a hard rock bottom, and sometimes that bottom was unbelievably low. As Dad described
it to me later, he would hit bedrock and keep on digging.
It was during the year 1967 that he was lower than he had ever
been before, and he most desperately needed my mother. He had
left Vivian by then, and he was touring with my mother. But she
refused to become involved with him romantically because he
was so drugged and crazy.

My father set off to visit some land he had purchased in
southeast Tennessee near Chattanooga, a place called Nicka-
jack Cave. He stumbled into the cave, stoned out of his mind,
not really sure what he was doing, but clearly suicidal. Inside the

cave over the next few hours he sobered up, and when he did, his suicidal notions abated with the high.

"I was scared out of my mind when I straightened up, son," he told me. "When I walked in that cave, only my guitar in my hand—not even a flashlight—I didn't know if I wanted to live or die. Then suddenly I was sober and knew for sure that I wanted to live. I wandered around for a long time in that cave, thought I was lost for good, that I would die there. And so I prayed. I begged God to let me find my way out. I promised Him I would change. It was not long after that I saw the light of the moon through the darkness."

When he came out of the cave, he still struggled with the drugs. But his love for my mother was unwavering. When he begged for her love in return, she gave him an ultimatum: "Either you straighten up, or I will leave the show and there will be no chance for anything between you and me." And so my father did that. He straightened up. Their love became strong, but I feel it never would have lasted if they had not experienced hardship and pain. For them complacency was as dangerous to their relationship as infidelity would have been. It was the uncertainty and excitement of it all that kept them interested.

And so my father, not long sober, asked my mother to marry him live while onstage in London, Ontario, the night of February 22, 1968. With the whole audience watching, he implored her to be his wife. And after some unstaged consideration, my mother finally said yes. I am eternally grateful that she did.

And so it was that two years after their marriage, almost to the day, I was born. At the time my father had a hit television show on ABC, and they brought me onstage in front of the world. It was into this life I was born, the limelight and excitement of superstardom, and it was in this world that I searched, grew, and struggled beside them.

My father was a solid rock when I was a little boy. He had given up drugs and it seemed the darkness was all in the past. I remember seeing him onstage in Washington, D.C., in 1976, reciting his famous poem "Ragged Old Flag." Back then to me, my father may as well have been the president himself—strong and true and larger than life. But at the same time, Dad was a gentle and loving man, my best friend. He taught me not only about life on the road but also about the woods and nature. From my dad I learned how to hunt squirrels and fish at an early age. My father was not into competitive sports in the least, only outdoor activities. And beyond all that, he taught me about people, showing me that folks are mainly good, and that most can be trusted.

Dad stayed close to Rosanne, Kathy, Cindy, and Tara, and they visited often, although all four of the girls grew up living with their mother in California. My mother's daughters, Carlene and Rosie, were both living in our home in Tennessee when I was born; however, Carlene married Joe Simpkins in 1971, and Rosie married Scott Lawhead in 1974. So by the time I was four years old, I was living for the most part as an only child. My father loved all his children equally; there was no doubt about it. But his marriage to my mother and my birth brought him peace. It seemed he had found his place and for the time being stopped searching.

Dad treasured his time at home with his family. While we were apart during my parents' long tours, he would write me letters regularly. I recall waiting for my parents to return home on the scheduled arrival day from a long tour, waiting and waiting. When the door finally opened and I heard the fall of his footsteps, I would run to meet him. Dad's eyes were full of light and joy, always gentle.

Dad and Mom were late one winter night, traveling home by bus from Wisconsin. I am not sure what year it was, but I was young, maybe six or seven. A great storm had settled in, and the snow was blowing hard—three inches on the ground in Nashville, which for our southern town is a great deal. The locals were unaccustomed to this type of weather. I waited eagerly with Winifred Kelly, whom I called K, for their arrival. As the night wore on I grew more and more worried, but also increasingly sleepy.

Finally, K put me to sleep in my bed, long past my bedtime. In the middle of the night I woke up, walked out of my bedroom and up to my parent's bedroom. It was still empty. Why weren't they home by now? I was afraid they had been in an accident. I looked outside and saw that it was still snowing. I sat down beside the front door and leaned my head up against the wall. Before long I drifted off to sleep.

When I awoke, I was back in my bed. I ran upstairs and found my parents asleep. I went to the kitchen where I smelled bacon cooking, and K at the stove. I saw two other people there I did not know.

It turns out the tour bus had gotten stuck at an exit ramp somewhere in Kentucky, its tires lodged in the deep, slushy snow. A couple driving a jeep had stopped to help them. When they realized it was my parents in the bus, they of course were surprised.

"We are trying to get back to see our son," Dad said.

"Well, we can take you," the man responded.

"That's a long drive," Dad said. "If you take us home, you will have to spend the night and eat breakfast with us."

And so it wasn't long until my parents came down to the kitchen, and we all ate breakfast. I remember those people were sweet and not pushy at all, or in the least bit starstruck. When we finished breakfast, they went on their way.

Dad and Mom were good-hearted, unassuming people. They had welcoming natures and offered their home in gratitude to these ordinary, helpful people.

Around 1979 something began to change, and though I did not understand it then, I do now. My father had begun to use drugs again and was struggling. The fights began, and I was usually right in the middle, literally and figuratively. The father that I had known as a boy began to dissolve into another man whom I did not know at all. Though the real John R. Cash, my dad, did come around quite often, "CASH," as my dad called him, also reared his ugly head with frequency. My mother's and father's love for one another altered and faded during these trying times, though it never disappeared.

One day during a particularly tough fight, I decided to shift the focus to me, as I did often. I ran outside while they were screaming at each other and called out, "I will never come back!"

I ran up a hill near our house on Caudill Drive in Hendersonville, Tennessee, and hid behind a bush. Within minutes my mother came up the hill.

"Son," she said, "we are sorry you are having to hear this." She put her arm around me and I cried and cried. I walked back down to the house with her, where my father sat waiting. They did not fight any more that day.

Though the fights got worse before things got better, and though my mother almost left my father during that period, their love simply would not die. My father's addiction had a strong hold on him, and some days he was simply not there—I mean both emotionally and mentally. I remember worrying that they would get a divorce, a horrible fear to me, second only to their dying. Like most children, I thought of my parents and myself as a unit, a being in itself. I saw that unit crumbling, and I was terrified, fearing my father might die. And it was this ongoing dance of fear that made it so hard. One day they were together and I saw hope for our family, but soon they were fighting horribly. The cadence of their marriage was not consistent in any way throughout my early teenage years.

The bottom came in 1983, when my father went to a hospital for a surgery to remove a cyst from within his sternum that was threatening to block his esophagus. When he came around from that surgery, after almost dying, the family gathered around him and begged him to get treatment. He did so. He wrote me a letter from the Betty Ford Center in Rancho Mirage, California.

Rancho Mirage, Ca.
B.F.C.
Dec. 21, 1983

Hi Son;
I have achieved another step. I am out of the Eisenhower Hosp.
and into the Betty Ford Center.
I'm very happy here. They are keeping me busy with all the
daily and evening activities.
I went to a lecture this morning. It was on meditation. I think
I'm learning how to meditate. Definition; Meditate: "The listening
half of prayer."
Isn't that neat?
Have a nice holiday son. I love and miss you and mama.
Dad

Later in my life I also suffered from addiction. Many had
assumed that after being so close to the darkness of my father's
addiction, I would not fall prey to this sickness myself. Addiction
holds no regard for the past, as we do. It was much greater than I
was and took hold of my life completely, as it did my father's. Dad
was one person when under the influence of drugs and another
when he was not.

I believe most assuredly that Dad was a good man, a strong
man, and a man of faith. But he was full of contradictions. Many
times in his life, the dark side overshadowed his true nature. He
would have been the first to say it was his selfish nature, the sin-
ner inside, that was in a seemingly eternal battle for control. And

though his faith was strong throughout his whole life, his darkness was forever his unwelcome companion, pulling him back into the same addictions and struggles.

So what pulled him through? Was it my mother's love for him, gentle and steadfast? Was it the fact that he had hit a hard bottom where his only chance of survival was to rise up? Was it his enduring faith in God? His desire to return to the fold and be that family man again? My belief is that it was all of these things.

It was the people in Dad's life, there to support him, who mattered. There were too many to do them justice here. There was never a time that Billy Graham wasn't there for Dad, always nonjudgmental, always caring. Larry Gatlin, Kris and Lisa Kristofferson, Waylon Jennings, Jessi Colter, and Dad's sister Reba Hancock were also there for him, and, of course, my mother.

When Dad returned from the Betty Ford Center, he had a new lease on life, a new direction. Like the Apostle Paul, the scales were pulled from his eyes.

So much has been written about his sickness and addiction. But they did not make the man. Each and every time it seemed diffused, the light within my father would come back, and that is how I remember him best. Yes, the light shined through and triumphed in the end. And that light was brightest when it was enhanced by my mother's. She was strong and at the same time just as gentle as the breeze from across the mountains where she was raised.

My father adored my mother, always did. He was a hard-headed old-fashioned man, for sure. And there were times when he could be hard on my mother, though never physically abusive—never to her, and never to me or any of the family. I remember many times when I was young my mother would roll her eyes at me and say, "Your dad is a BEAR today!" But she had a way of softening his toughness, reducing his stress, and making life easier on him. In the process, she made life easier on all of us.

That gentle love Dad had for Mom was evident in the many letters he wrote to her through the years. And not only letters. Dad would give personalized gifts to her, perhaps a photo album with handwritten captions and anecdotal comments around the photos. Dad always took the time that was needed to show my mother in concrete ways how much he loved her, and certainly his actions were paramount in keeping their love strong and fresh all through the years.

My parents certainly had their struggles through the years, but their love remained strong. They always found their way back to each other. Their life was not necessarily "happily ever after" but rather "happy after all."

CHAPTER FIVE

THE HOUSE ON THE LAKE

It was a cold winter day and a pot of chili—my father's recipe—was simmering on the stove. He walked by the pot and threw a handful of self-rising cornmeal into it, or really, he threw it at the pot. Most of the cornmeal did not make it into the pot but rather scattered all over the stove, and more than a little landed on the floor below. Dad's recipe for chili contained a few unusual ingredients, one of which was self-rising cornmeal. Later in life he stopped making the chili himself, but he always made sure to add his own special touches. His methods were not always graceful, however.

"Stir it up, Kti!" he said with a smile to the cook, who rolled her eyes at him in annoyance. She did stir, albeit not dutifully.

Dad was a great cook, in his own inimitable way. In addition to chili, he had a repertoire of home-style dishes, including fried chicken.

When I was young, my father and I would go to his farm in Bon Aqua in Hickman County, Tennessee. We would stop at the grocery on the way and stock up.

After we had carried the groceries and overnight bags into the farmhouse, Dad would grab his shotgun and we would take to the woods. Usually we came back with a rabbit and a squirrel, plenty to eat for the two of us. Dad would clean our kill and put the cut-up pieces in saltwater to draw out the blood. Then he would roll the pieces in flour and salt and pepper and fry in Crisco until golden brown, always in a cast-iron skillet. After the game was fried up, he would make gravy out of the leftover grease and spoon this concoction on top of biscuits.

In the morning it was usually fried eggs, sausage, more biscuits, and gravy, this time sausage gravy.

Peanuts were for snacks, and Dad always roasted his own. He would grab a hunk of skin on his arm and pinch it as he chewed. "See that, son?" he would say, gesturing toward his arm. "See that? Peanuts. You are what you eat." Then he would laugh.

Lunch was fried bologna with white bread and mustard. Dinner, if it wasn't game or chili, was frozen pizzas. Not exactly a healthy diet, but this was the way the man ate when he was the one behind the stove.

Old Bon Aqua Iron Pot was what Dad called his chili. Sometimes he called it Black Bart, although I have no idea why. When he cooked it himself, it was an all-day affair. He would sweat over the stove for hours, chopping onions, his eyes watering. The steak was cut up in large chunks, the cans of beans scattered about the kitchen, and, of course, the cornmeal was all over the place. Now I make the same chili, which is mostly unchanged from Dad's original recipe.

A little Cash family chili philosophy. Chili is an art, and to master it you have to go beyond the recipe. The recipe is not a formula; it's only a guide. Dad believed that even the best recipe should be adapted to the cook's taste.

Although Mom was the better cook, Dad was not afraid to give it all he had, and his creativity showed in many ways. He was adept at frying foods, truly his favorite method of preparation. He made fried chicken, fried turkey breast strips, country-fried steak, fried catfish, and, of course, fried squirrel and rabbit.

When Dad got older, his love for fried foods and the like did not dwindle, but he was happy to let someone else do the frying. He grew accustomed to our Sunday visits and expected my wife, Laura, and I to bring fried chicken each time. We brought over the grandchildren and the fried chicken. If for some reason we could not make it, both my parents were sorely disappointed.

Dad liked his chicken extra crispy. First he would remove the fried skin off his portion and eat it. Only then would he try a bite or two of the chicken.

Dad's fried dishes were not the norm in our house when I was growing up. But there was always plenty of food. Some of my family's favorite dishes were tomato gravy with homemade biscuits, Mom's "stuff" (a combination of potatoes and other vegetables fried in a pan, and then finished off with hot pepper cheese), and "son of a bitchin' stew," which was my grandfather Ezra's creation. It contained various meats and vegetables—everything the icebox had to offer.

My parents were endlessly creative in the kitchen. During the 1990s, one of the family favorites was Cashburgers.

Although Dad enjoyed cooking at the farm in Bon Aqua, most of the cooking, living, and loving took place at the House on the Lake. It was home, the heart of my parents' lives. Dad stumbled on the house accidentally.

After leaving Vivian and moving to Tennessee, Dad was living in Madison in an apartment not too far away from my mother's home. His roommate was Waylon Jennings. Since they both spent a lot of time on the road, they were able to give each other enough space. If they had been in such close quarters all the time, I doubt their friendship would have lasted. Dad told me that two men should never live together, that it would ruin their friendship. As far as I know, since Dad's time in the air force, Waylon was his one and only male roommate.

So in 1967 Dad went to find a place to call his own and discovered it at 200 Caudill Drive in Hendersonville, just north of Nashville. Dad bought the home from its builder, Braxton Dixon, in 1967 while on an excursion to investigate the lakeside lots in the area.

The story goes that Dad pulled up in his Cadillac and walked straight up to Braxton.

"Do you plan on this being your home?" he asked.

"It will be when I'm finished with it," Braxton responded.

Dad shook his head with a smile. "No, it will be my home," he responded.

"Sorry, but no," said Braxton.

Dad pulled out his checkbook. "Name the price," he said.

And so Braxton relented eventually and sold the property to my father, who also bought the surrounding one hundred and fifty acres.

TOP | *The House on the Lake as I knew it growing up, grand and magnificent.*

BOTTOM | *This is a photograph of the ruin of the House on the Lake as it stood in 2011. When I heard about the house burning, it felt to me like someone had died, and I grieved for quite some time.*

I remember the home I lived in as a boy and teenager fondly. It was a welcoming place, with wide and tall windows and high ceilings (the master bedroom's was over twenty feet tall). All three floors were packed full of furniture, mostly Renaissance Revival pieces from the nineteenth century. My mother would brag that in all of their homes put together there were over eighty beds (though many of them were dismantled). There were a goodly few strewn throughout the House on the Lake.

When we weren't touring, summer brought lazy days spent swimming and cooking out. I can visualize the doorjamb where my height was notched as I grew. My father's height was also marked to show when I passed his six foot one inches at the age of fifteen. I remember the round bedroom that was mine, where I had set up a drum set on the wooden frame of the round bed in its center. My rock band would play loud music, my parents ever patient and always allowing us to crank it up.

I recall the quiet Sunday mornings, long before there was cable, sitting with my parents and reading the Bible, while our coonhound Molly curled up on the living room couch. She was the only dog my mother ever allowed in any of her houses.

The House on the Lake was mostly a happy place. Dad loved to laugh; he had a great sense of humor. Though good friends with Elvis Presley, Dad often did a silly impersonation of him on his show during the 1950s. Elvis returned the compliment by imitating my father on some of his own live shows.

Dad had friends who loved him dearly and wanted nothing from him but his friendship. They were producers, musicians, farmers, and businessmen. When I think of these easygoing relationships, the first person who comes to mind is "Cowboy" Jack Clement. Cowboy first met Dad at Sun Records in 1956. He was the original engineer on many of Dad's early recordings and also penned a few of Dad's early hits.

Dad laughed and told jokes with Cowboy and sometimes was just plain silly. I remember seeing Dad at the Cowboy Arms Hotel and Recording Spa dressed in a top hat, with a child's pig-nose disguise around his face. He was carrying a small amplifier on a shoulder strap while playing guitar. Cowboy would join in and they would dance around the studio.

Other dear friends at the "spa" were David Ferguson (Dad's longtime engineer), Chance Martin, and Jim Varney. There were a host of others, too many to mention, who also frequented the studio.

Times were fun during the 1980s for Dad, especially from 1984 on. He made a lot of great music at Cowboy's studio during that period. Although Dad was dropped by Columbia in 1986, he didn't let this stifle his creativity. Some have argued that the 1980s were a low point, but Dad did some great work with Cowboy, including the album *Water from the Wells of Home*, which consisted of duets with everyone from Paul McCartney to Roy Acuff.

Each Christmas we would have parties, and family and friends would come from around the country, or the world sometimes, to join us. At the time Mom's daughter Carlene was married to rocker Nick Lowe, and the couple lived in England. Nick would bring his bandmates and friends. Other holiday season visitors included Elvis Costello, Tom Petty, the Heartbreakers, and Bono and Adam Clayton from U2.

When I left home at the age of eighteen, I was certain that I was my own man and unaware that I was not done growing up. I saw my mother cry as I walked out the door, my belongings in my arms as I headed for my first apartment. I remember Mom and Dad both saying "You always have a place at home, son," their eyes sad but strong.

But later, when I was lost, I remember trying to go back and finding that the novelist Thomas Wolfe was correct: You can never go home again. Nevertheless, through the years that house was a beacon. I created another home eventually, but I truly believe that in our heart of hearts, our family home is our true home. I will always remember it that way.

After my parents passed, the family estate sold the house and lakeside lot to Barry Gibb of the Bee Gees. It was in great need of some work to restore it to its original splendor, and Barry and his wife, Linda, renovated the house. After months of work, the place was two weeks away from moving day.

On April 10, 2007, I was in Oregon with my wife and family. I was driving across the Yaquina Bay Bridge in Newport when my phone rang. It was the entertainer and musician Marty Stuart, a longtime friend of my father's who at one time had been married to my sister Cindy.

When I answered, I heard the desperation in Marty's voice. "It's burning down, John Carter," he said. I felt a chill as I pulled over to the side of the road beyond the bridge. "I'm watching it burn to the ground. They are trying to put the fire out, but it's too far gone."

I sat and cried on the phone with Marty that day. Losing that house was for me like losing a loved one. Its demise signaled the passing of an age. The House on the Lake had been destined to be home to only one family: the Cashes.

CHAPTER SIX

RAINBOW-COLORED GLASSES

ad was a huge fan of the painter and sculptor Frederic Remington and had a few original castings of his bronzes, plus a sketchbook of his doodles. But Dad's style was not influenced in the least by Remington, or any other painter. Art was not something that Dad studied, and he never attempted to copy any technique. He probably could not have told you whether his style was inspired by surrealism, or abstract expressionism, or any other art movement. Instead, art was a very personal therapy to him, something he cherished, but not as most artists do. It was almost as if each work he painted was in some way simply an extension of his signature. Much of it resembled lines and colors splashed across a white canvas. But it is undeniable that he expressed his emotions and state of mind in this art. From the first time I saw my dad's drawings and paintings, I have been enthralled.

My dad's lifelong love of sketching and doodling began at an early age. His humor and unique sense of irony are evident in these drawings.

In the early 1990s, Dad's jaw was broken when a bone shattered during a particularly intense dental surgery. There was massive nerve damage, and he was in horrific agony. A bone graft was done, and his jaw was wired shut, forcing Dad to cancel his tours for an extended period. During the prolonged recovery, a doctor suggested he purchase a writing pad and pastels and put his pains down on the page. I am not sure if this helped relieve the pain itself, but it certainly gave him a release.

Art was therapy to him. Even at the end of his life, he used the pen as a form of self-expression, a way to put his suffering and pains on paper.

Throughout his life, my father always had a tremor in his hand, which was noticeable in his handwriting and also his art. But he used it to his advantage, adding dynamic intensity to his style. His Christian studies led him to pull out charcoal or pen and express his excitement about his faith in works such as *Armageddon*, a dark and foreboding vision of the apocalypse, and *The Shroud*, a charcoal representation of the supposed face of Christ, drawn from the Shroud of Turin.

Dad painted not to prove anything but to express himself. There were those who supported Dad's art, the aforementioned doctor being one. And I certainly must express gratitude to Dad's dear friend Bill Miller for his encouragement of my father. It was Bill who suggested he paint his only work that we have on a large canvas, which is called *Flight*.

I remember Dad drawing, his pastel pencils out, making his scribbles and streaks chaotically across the pages. He would slash five or six brush strokes across the easel and then glare at his work, attempting to decipher it. More often than not, he would wad the paper up and throw it in the trash. Sometimes he would set the painting in a stack and move on to the next.

My father was a contemplative man.

My father had a Leicaflex camera, and during the 1970s, he was a prolific photographer. Chance Martin, an employee of my father's at the time, remembers Dad buying this camera in Germany in 1976. According to Chance, what got Dad interested in photography was a fan book that Chance had put together for Dad. Chance, a photographer himself, had published a few of his own photos in this book, which was sold on the road show as a souvenir.

He introduced Dad to macro photography on a two-week trip to my family's vacation home in Jamaica, Cinnamon Hill Great House. With a macro lens, a photographer can take very close-up shots of tiny subjects, which look huge in the final shot. Dad took a great many photos on this trip to Jamaica with Chance at his side. He photographed every small object he could get close to—skulls, bats, scorpions, and flowers. Despite his tremor, Dad held a steady hand for these shots. He also took many great photos of landscapes and, of course, of people—people he loved and those he found intriguing. He had a way of seeing the story in their eyes and capturing it with his camera. Dad had a photographer's magical eye. He mostly used only natural light, adjusting his camera's aperture as necessary.

It was a sight to see when Dad was on one of his shoots. He sometimes would go out from a hotel, whether it was in a small European town or in New York City, his camera around his neck and his bag over his shoulder. I would follow.

One day when we were in London, walking through Piccadilly Circus, we stopped so that he could take some shots of architecture.

"My goodness," called a lady who watched the photographer beside me. "Are you Johnny Cash?"

Dad put the camera down and smiled back at her.

"Why, yes, Mum, I am," he said.

The lady fumbled in her purse for her camera. By the time she raised it, Dad had beaten her to the punch, holding up his own and snapping a shot of her before she could get him.

He laughed and we both posed for her photo.

CHAPTER SEVEN

FROM HEART TO PEN

ad's thoughts and words seemed to take the most direct route from his heart to pen and paper. He had a simple, honest style that none could match. He was amazingly prolific, too, and wrote throughout his life. When things were good, he wrote. When he was struggling—whether with physical pain, relationship issues, or addiction—he wrote. When he was alone and searching for the inner peace he needed, he wrote. Pen and paper were his constant companions all the days of his life.

Dad knew what he wanted to do with his life most certainly when he returned from the air force. He was determined to pursue music, although perhaps this was not a choice. Maybe the music simply had to come out. Perhaps his poetry and songs were his very lifeblood, somehow predestined to emerge during his lifetime and lead his spirit onward.

Dad was endlessly creative and energetic, always pursuing a fresh idea for a song that caught his heart. Of course, he will be most remembered for his most famous compositions, including "Folsom Prison Blues," "I Walk the Line," and "Hey Porter," to name a few. But it is the creative process that intrigues me the most. A man like my father is remembered by his successes and not by his failures, and he had a great deal of both. But even the fragments of his unfinished works can give one insight into his unique method of creativity.

Dad found inspiration for his music easily. Much of his writing was introspective. In "I Walk the Line," for example, he examined his dedication to his mate. He revised his songs a great deal, but more often than not, his initial from-the-gut concept was what he settled with in the end.

To my father, poetry—like painting and photography—was an avenue for free self-expression. He held to no rule or principle, except to let the ink flow. His spirit controlled the process completely.

My father and I wrote the song "Death and Hell" together. It had an unusual source of inspiration for sure. We were traveling on the bus between shows during a series of one-night stands. Dad read in the newspaper a very unusual scientific study: It had been determined that when a cat fell from a window three to nine stories high, it would normally die upon landing because its body was tense and the cat felt the full impact of the fall. However, if the cat fell out of a window more than nine stories high, it had enough time to stretch out and relax its limbs and torso, which helped it survive. We laughed about this all day. Dad had also read somewhere that according to an old wives' tale, pigs can see the wind. Inspired by these two unique bits of information, we developed the chorus for the song "Death and Hell." The main story came from our imaginations. It was recorded on the High-waymen album *The Road Goes on Forever.*

Mom lovingly watches Dad. She always saw the light and goodness in every situation.

One song that comes to mind when talking about my dad's creative process is "The Man Comes Around," which appears on the album *American IV*. I recall the first day Dad showed me the song. The concept for the song had come to him in a dream, a very unusual one. In his dream he entered Queen Elizabeth's court and humbly approached the throne. She looked up at him and said, "You're like a thorn tree in a whirlwind."

He awoke wondering what this could mean and began to study the Scriptures, certain that he would find the solution there. This began the process of writing the song that is arguably one of the greatest compositions of his later life.

Dad called me and asked that I come to his office and hear a new song. I arrived, and after a short visit with my mother, went to see Dad. He was sitting at his desk, and there on his table were at least twenty sheets. Some of the papers were just short fragments of lyrics, and some were longer versions, but they were all various notations and versions of "The Man Comes Around."

Dad picked up his guitar. "Hey, thanks for coming by so soon. I want to play you this new song," he said eagerly. The excitement in his voice was clear.

And so he began to strum and sing the song. As I remember, it was note for note and lyrically exactly the version we wound up with as the final recording.

"Wow, Dad," I said as he finished. "That is unbelievable. I love the part about 'virgins trimming their wicks.'"

His eyes lit up again. He reached and picked up his Bible. It was always on his desk. "Let me show you. That is a parable of sorts. Aren't you familiar with it?" I had to admit I wasn't. He showed me the Scripture, opening to the twenty-fifth chapter of Matthew. As he read out loud, I looked more closely at the sheets of paper on his desk. There were a good few additional verses.

When he finished reading, I asked him what those pages were. "Oh, when I get onto a good thing that I'm excited about, I just keep writing. Those are various versions that I may include in the song."

Later, while recording, Dad did try a few of these verses. But the original version was the strongest. The exciting burst of inspiration that resulted in this song was so important to him.

Dad had asthma and battled it through the last few years of his life. But his persistence and ability to laugh at his own mortality stayed with him. Dad was in and out of the hospital with pneumonia quite often the last year of his life. Not two months before he died, he began to work on "Like the 309," a song that shows perseverance and humor in the face of death, and which can be heard on *American V*.

Through each and every stage of his life, the man always wrote and made music. It was his career but also his life's therapy, his very breath and blood. Though life doled out pain and suffering, loss and solitude, his creativity endured.

CHAPTER EIGHT

A STANDARD
OF
COMPARISON

PAGE 94: My father always had a deep sense of peace and connection to God. His music and faith were especially important to him in his later years.

ad learned his great love of the sea from my grandfather Ezra Carter. Our home in Port Richey, Florida, just north of Tampa, had belonged to Maybelle and Ezra from the mid-1960s until their deaths in the 1970s. (This spacious home stayed in the family until 2002.) My grandfather was unafraid of the ocean and had once been stranded out in the ocean for two days. His boat was only a fifteen-foot skiff. The tale goes that when the Coast Guard found him, alone and washed out who knows how far from shore, he had his fishing pole in hand, and he was laughing and still trying to fill his cooler with fish. I was fascinated by his hearty nature and wanted to be just like him. As it turned out, Dad and I would have our own adventure.

There was a citrus orchard in the backyard of our Florida home, which Dad took great pleasure in, pruning the trees and reaping the harvest every summer. We were there a lot. He loved the weather and the sun. We had friends, the Littles, who had a house built on stilts in the shallow ocean just beyond the Pithlachascotee River channel. Our home was on the Cotee, as the locals called it. Dad had numerous guests come stay with us there, including Billy and Ruth Graham. The friends, the orchard, and the sun were great, but our place in Florida was about one thing, really: fishing. We fished all the time. We set out chum lines for sharks and mackerel, but mostly we just went bottom fishing.

This story, as I remember it, is 100 percent true. We were sitting on the bridge of our twenty-five-foot not-quite-seaworthy boat and headed out into the great Gulf of Mexico, as we had every day that week. I was twelve that summer of 1982. Like my granddad, my father had no fear of the sea. We would go thirty or forty miles out, with no view of land in sight and with nothing but a two-way radio, which worked sometimes and at other times did not.

That day we were heading out into the Gulf, its waters completely still. There wasn't a cloud in the sky. We had heard a report that some scattered thunderstorms might arrive in the afternoon, but we were used to that. In the great expanse of the ocean, we could pick out the storms on the horizon and avoid them. Or at least this had worked before.

The fishing was good that day and we pulled in a diverse bounty. I was amazed at the variety of life to be found in the warm waters of the Gulf. We caught grunts, lips, black bass, snakefish, sand sharks, sand dabbers, dogfish, triggerfish, blowfish, tilefish, hogfish, and, of course, grouper, which, of all these, was the fish we wanted most. Things were different back then, and if there were limits on what or how much we could catch, we were unaware of them. We kept everything, putting live fish in the holding tank of the boat, where fresh water poured through all day, keeping them alive or at least fresh.

The day wore on and we kept fishing. We were not anchored and floated around with the motor turned off, bottom fishing. This method was quite successful back then—there were many fish. We would go for a while and not get a bite, and then suddenly for fifteen minutes, we were catching fish after fish. Lots of fun, just a man and his son, forty miles out, no GPS or cell phone. And that was one of those days when the radio wasn't working.

I noticed a cloud on the horizon, thick, black, and dangerous looking, but far away. I looked at Dad and saw that he was looking at the same cloud.

"Well, son," he said, beginning to reel in his rod, "I s'pose we had best be heading back in."

I looked out toward the end of my rod and saw that there was, unbelievably, a small yellow bird on the tip.

"Look, Dad!" I cried. "Look at the little bird!"

He looked and smiled. "I guess we have a visitor, son. A finch. Wonder what he's doing so far out here?"

"I just don't know," I said, holding my rod tightly so as not to jerk the bird about. "Do you think he'll stay with us all the way back?" I asked.

Dad smiled. "Maybe so," he answered. "Now you best pull in your line." The wind had picked up in the past few minutes, causing the previously tranquil sea to ripple and rise in small swells. I felt a gusting breeze rise to my face, my hair blowing.

"Well, okay," I said, and began to crank up the reel.

To my surprise the little bird stayed on the tip of my pole. Dad went over to the cockpit to start the boat, but when he turned the key, there was no sound at all.

"Well, what on earth?" he said, trying again, but still getting no response from the motor.

When I pulled in my line and set my rod down, the bird flew up and disappeared.

"What's wrong, Dad?"

"I just don't know, son. I just don't know."

My father was no mechanic. He could not tell you the difference between a radiator and a carburetor. He just had no understanding of machinery at all.

The wind was blowing strong now. "Well," he said reluctantly, "I guess I had better take a look."

And so he went back and opened the engine well, lay down on his stomach, and looked down into the oily compartment below, puzzled. I was on my knees beside him. I thought I smelled smoke. "Well, son, looks like we are just going to have to fix it ourselves," he said, but his tone betrayed the uncertainty he felt.

He got down in the belly of that boat and dug around in the darkness with just a penlight. He had a brand-new wrench, never before used, and with it he tightened the battery cables and knocked lightly on the spark plugs, trying everything his limited knowledge suggested.

"Son!" he called from the depths of the boat. "Son, try to start the engine!"

The wind was blowing hard now, and the boat was rocking steadily.

I turned the key, but still the engine made no sound.

"Nothing, Dad!" I cried.

"Well, dag-gum it!" he called in response.

Something caught my eye. I saw the little yellow bird again, now roosting on the starboard gunwales, close to the bow.

"Dad, the little bird is back," I called.

"Yes, he's most surely here to help," he answered.

I went back to the engine well and looked down. I could see my dad's posterior sticking out of a corner of the motor, the rest of his body obscured by the dark engine well. I heard a slam of metal on metal. "There's a cable undone back here; just can't get it back on." Again the metallic clanking sound, followed by another "Dag-gum!" Then came more grunting and finally a sigh of accomplishment. "There!" said Dad, exasperated. "Now give it a try."

As I went back to the wheel, I saw the little bird again, this time sitting on the port stern. I looked up and saw that the storm was now almost upon us, blowing our little boat about in what was now becoming a very rough sea. I sat down at the helm, said a prayer, and turned the key.

With a cough, the engine rumbled to life.

"Well, alright!" I heard Dad call from below.

He climbed out of the engine well and over to the helm, taking the wheel. And then we were off, as fast as our little boat could go, heading east.

I looked back to see if the little bird was still sitting on the stern of the boat, but it was gone. We went on, the sea beating at the sides of the boat, the wind beginning to pelt us with rain, the waves ever higher.

When we slowed the boat down because of the rising seas, a movement caught my eye. There out beside the boat I saw the little yellow bird, flying fast to keep up with us.

"The bird!" I cried.

Dad looked and sure enough, there was the little bird, flying right beside us.

"Dad! It wants to be on the boat with us!"

Dad smiled. "I am sure it will be just fine," he said.

I watched that little bird for the longest time as it flew just above the waves. The wind was gusting mightily now, and the rain was pelting down. Still the little bird continued beside our vessel, beating its tiny wings with all its strength.

We crested a great wave, and our boat crashed back down, the bow hitting the sea forcefully. We both fell forward, struggling to keep our balance. Dad straightened the boat back into the wind, which luckily was from the northeast that day, and we slowed even more.

When I looked up again the little bird was gone.

"Dad!" I cried. "The bird! The bird is gone! It went down in the waves!" Tears were beginning to well up in my eyes.

Over the roar of the wind he answered, "Son, that bird is fine. I am sure it was a guardian to watch over us. We are safe, now. The bird is gone on."

And so we kept on, and before long the wind began to die down, and with it, the tumultuous seas. As the clouds departed and the waves subsided, I saw that land was in fact not as far away as I had believed. Before long we were in the channel and soon at the dock. It was almost dark.

We had fried fish that night, made with my mother's recipe. It was wonderful. But as I lay down to sleep, exhausted and beaten by the sun, sea, and wind, I could not get that little bird out of my mind.

There were so many times when we were in dangerous places, so many times when I feared for my life. But I always felt safe. How is this so? I believed. Was the bird a guardian? Was I truly safe because of a spirit watching over us? Or was I safe with the man I trusted and believed in? Perhaps both. But maybe it was my dad's faith that reassured me, rather than my own. There were many times when I was uncertain and afraid. But Dad believed. His faith was strong.

A lesson taught with words and force is seldom learned. This I learned from Dad through his words and actions. I have learned my lessons in only two ways: by watching the example of others or through my own pains, my own wrong turns. No one could make me believe I was not on the right path if I did not want to believe it. I had to take it and find out for myself. My father was the same way. Though he suffered many times from his addictions, bad choices, and bad living, he would return again and again to the same path, only to find the same results. It was many years before he made positive, lasting changes.

When I was suffering from addiction and in great emotional pain, I went to my father. In 1991, when I was barely twenty-one, I was lost and scared, depressed and needing help. Dad was never angry with me over my addiction, just hurt and concerned. He told me I had a great faith, that this faith was in my blood, and that my salvation was already determined. He reminded me of my ancestors, how my great-grandfather, grandfather, and he were all ordained ministers, and this faith in Christ was in my soul. In this I found strength and understanding. My father prayed with me that day. Both of us admitted that we were lost and alone, needed help, and needed each other. We prayed for God to give us strength, to show us His way. I believe that God was there with us that day, that He heard our prayer and that in His own way and time, He answered it.

But sadly, neither my nor my father's addictions passed immediately with that prayer. Before long I was as lost as I'd ever been. Within a year, my father and I both went to another drug treatment center, this time less than a month apart.

In the summer of 1992, Dad finished his in-treatment program and moved into a rental house, continuing his extended treatment. I came to join Dad at the house, and at his urging, I went in for evaluation and family therapy. I was pretending to be off drugs, but in reality was still using. I had stopped drinking, but was smoking grass and taking Xanax. I attended a group session at the center one day and expressed my great anger in front of the group, which came out in the form of incoherent ranting. I spoke out against the addiction in our family as if I was not experiencing it myself, as if I had been a victim. I went back to the rental house that evening in a huff.

The counselor, a tough, stern, and wise man, reached out to my father and told him of my outburst. Dad came to me that night and we had a long talk. I was no longer angry, but still I was upset. I also told him I had not been using drugs.

Dad knew better. Before he went to bed he put the letter on the next page beneath my door.

—John C.

I'm not giving you this scripture to admonish you.

It's the one I read to you on the phone from Bon Aqua.

I needed to hear this more than you did.

Eccl. 5:2-3 "Be not rash with thy mouth and let not thine heart be hasty to utter anything before God: for God is in Heaven, and thou upon Earth: therefore let thy words be few.

For a dream cometh through a multitude of business; and a fools voice is known by multitude of words."

Love Dad

After I read the letter, I was still angry. I immediately wadded up the paper and threw it in the wastebasket. I lay on the bed for a while, staring at the ceiling and sifting through my jumbled thoughts. Then I got up and took the paper out of the wastebasket and reread it. As I lay there, I pondered what the letter meant. It was a way of reaching me without pointing a finger, without judging me. His letter was truly a gift, a way to reach out and show unconditional compassion. The next day I checked myself into the treatment center.

Dad was open-minded and understanding because he had experienced what I was going through. He hoped that those he loved would not suffer the same pains and struggles that he had, but when we did, he supported and stood by us. He also had the ability to see the miracles in what appeared to be commonplace; his faith helped those who loved him find greater strength and purpose. So many of us looked up to him. And when we were troubled, we reached out to him, knowing we would never be denied his wisdom or unconditional love.

CHAPTER NINE

NEW BEGINNINGS & LEGACIES

.

lthough Dad had never stopped being creative, the public was just not catching on. He was still selling tickets in the early 1990s, and the audiences still cheered. But he was not enjoying any hits, and he missed the excitement of bringing out new material to critical acclaim. His audience seemed to be getting older and older.

Then in February 1993, a man with long hair and an even longer beard showed up backstage at the Rhythm Café in Santa Ana, California, where Dad was playing. His name was Rick Rubin. Dad's manager, Lou Robin, had come to Dad before the show to tell him that Rick wanted to talk to him afterward.

"I'd say he's just another record company guy who wants to sell his ideas to me, but I'll meet him and at least hear him out," Dad had answered without a lot of enthusiasm.

And so Rick came into Dad's dressing room and both men said hello. Then, according to Lou, Rick and Dad simply sat and stared at each other for two minutes or so, saying nothing and seeming to size each other up. Dad figured Rick was probably looking for an easy gig with an established artist, but instead Rick proposed something Dad had always dreamed of but had never been offered: a simple recording plan. Come into the studio with me and make the music you have always wanted to make. Follow your heart, and record with a band or not. Sit in front of the microphone and sing your songs the way you want.

For Dad, this was a breath of fresh air compared to the options he could have found in Nashville or elsewhere from various producers. And so Dad signed the deal with Rick Rubin and his newly formed company, American Recordings. Dad went to Los Angeles and spent day after day at Rick's house, making the music his heart dictated.

Dad did record with a band some on that first trip to Rick's in 1993, but very little of that material was released. It was the simplest production, only voice and guitar, that was the focus of the first record with Rick, titled *American Recordings*, like the company's name. The songs were a varied assortment, from the dark and mysterious "Thirteen" to Dad's heartfelt version of Kris Kristofferson's "Why Me." But it was my father's arrangement of the old American murder ballad "Delia's Gone" that received the most acclaim. The video for the song, featuring the supermodel Kate Moss as the ill-fated young woman, portrayed my father as a dark and dangerous figure—her lover and her murderer. Americans loved it, including American youth, which was most exciting for my father. It wasn't long before Dad's career was on fire again.

Both *American Recordings* and its follow-up, *Unchained*, featuring Tom Petty and the Heartbreakers as the backing band, won Grammy Awards. But country radio and Nashville in general did not pay much heed.

I was having a quiet dinner with my parents one evening in 1996, not long after Dad's *Unchained* had won the Grammy for Best Country Album. Winning was a big deal for sure. "Well, I talked to Billy [Graham] today," Dad announced. "Just after I got a call from Rick. Rick wants to take out an ad in Billboard."

He chewed. "What kind of ad?" I asked.

"The huge kind," he replied, spooning out the corn bread from his cup of buttermilk. "The kind that will rattle things. He wants to use the finger photo."

One of the most famous photographs in existence is the "bird shot," as we call it around the family. The photo, taken at one of the rehearsals for the live concert at San Quentin, captures my father's spirit at its rebellious best.

"I said no at first," Dad continued, "then I called Billy Graham. He didn't tell me to do it or not to do it, just that he wouldn't judge me either way. After my talk with him, I prayed about it and called Rick back. I gave him the go-ahead."

The advertisement read: "American Recordings and Johnny Cash would like to acknowledge the Nashville Music establishment and country radio for your support."

Of course, this ad really shook Nashville up. In many ways it was a wake-up call. Perhaps country music was broader and more expansive than the power brokers in Nashville had assumed. It was after this ad was placed that country radio program directors and record company executives all over the world took note. Many of them had it framed and put on permanent display in their offices. It became a reminder to stay open-minded and pay attention to what the people wanted—to facilitate, rather than direct the music business. It was after this ad appeared that the genre of Americana took root and became firmly established in our culture. This movement owes a great deal to my father's records on American Recordings.

Dad retired from the road in 1997 due to his illnesses, but this did not slow down his music. He recorded more and more. When Dad began work on *American III*, he asked me to join him in the studio. Dad wanted to record music in his log cabin near the House on the Lake in Hendersonville. He had set up a small recording system there a few years before and had put down some songs. Now he wanted to make it more of an operating studio.

In fact, the only extended period he wasn't in the studio was the time he spent at either of my parents' two peaceful vacation homes. One, in Jamaica, was the fabulous Cinnamon Hill Great House. Cinnamon Hill, overlooking the beautiful Caribbean Sea two miles below, was built in the first half of the eighteenth century by the Barrett family. At one time it was the family residence on a huge sugarcane plantation. The home was a safe haven to my parents, where they could truly rest, the gentle trade winds blowing up from the ocean.

The second home-away-from-home was the Carter Family ancestral home in Hiltons, Virginia. It was built by Ezra Carter in the 1930s. My mother could trace her heart roots to this place and reaffirm her faith. Dad loved it, too. They spent hour after hour on the front porch, writing, reading, and making music.

But Dad couldn't stay away from the studio for long.

And so Dad had his engineer David Ferguson buy a bit more gear and wire the cabin up for professional recording. Often, Rick

My father's best friend was his brother Jack, two years his senior, who died at the age of fourteen.

My father at twelve years old.

As a child, my father listened to the Carter Family on the radio. Among the second generation of this illustrious musical family were my mother, June (middle), and her sisters Anita (left) and Helen (right).

Dad poses in his airforce uniform.

Eddie Hill, Dad, Porter Wagoner, and Hawshaw Hawkins in Meridian, Mississippi, in 1957.

Dad tuning a twelve string resonator guitar.

photos taken at home with Vivian Liberto, my Dad's wife at the time, in 1958 by Columbia Records photographer *...nstein, right after Dad signed with the label.*

Mom in full form as a character she created, Aunt Polly Carter.

The greatest love of my father's life was undeniably my mot June Carter. When they married on March 1, 1968, Dad w the slate clean and started anew. Certainly this was one of most important years in his life for many reasons.

Maybelle and the Carter Sisters with my father in the late 1960s.

I was born on March 3, 1970, two years after my parents' marriage.

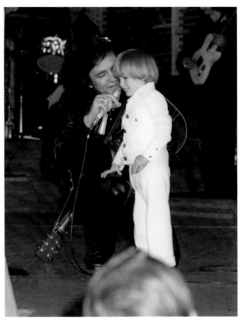

My father reaches down to share the microphone with a young me.

I never knew Tara (far left), Cindy (left), Kathy (right), and Rosanne (far right), my father's daughters from his marriage to Vivian Liberto, as half sisters, but only as whole ones. This feeling came from my parents, who wanted me to see no separation between us. Lifewise, I have always felt the same way about my mother's daughters, Rosie Nix Adams and Carlene Carter.

Throughout his life, my father was my absolute best friend.

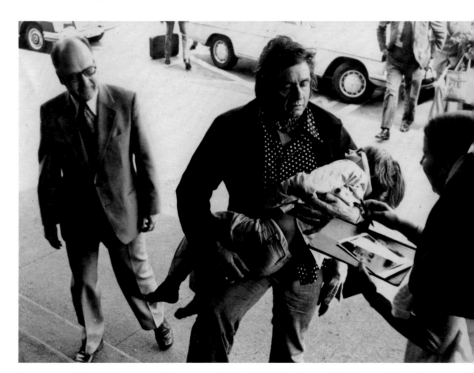

I never saw my father decline a request for an autograph, even when his hands were full (with me, in this case).

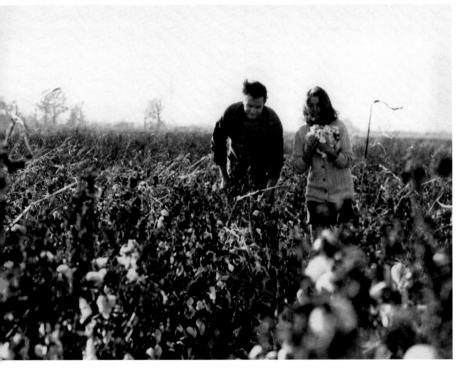

...y parents in the late 1960s on a visit to the cotton fields near Dad's childhood home in Dyess, Arkansas.

...n visits to Cinnamon Hill, Jamaica, my father would make time to care for orphans at the S.O.S. Children's Village in Barrett Town. My sisters, Rosie (left) and Rosanne (middle), sit behind my Dad in this photo.

Dad and Mom often had friends over for what Dad called "guitar pulls." The guitar was passed around and everyone played his or her newest compositions. The conversation often took an introspective turn.

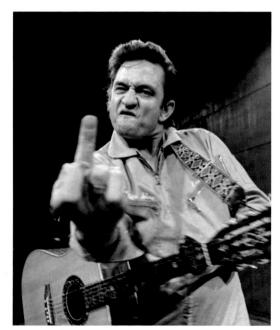

When American IV *won a Grammy Award, Rick suggested an advertisement featuring this famous photograph be taken out in* Billboard, *thanking the Nashville music establishment and country radio for their support. Dad was never afraid to express his emotions or strong feelings, however he saw fit.*

My parents' love for each other was indispensible, and it came through in their many performances together.

A final kiss always followed my parents' rousing performance of "Jackson."

My father used to call my mother "June Love."

...her and mother at home with each other in the House on the Lake.

...rary to his public image, Dad had quite a sense of humor and was always clowning around.

A "guitar pull" in the lakeside room at the House on the Lake. Here, Dad, Kris Kristofferson (second from right), and Chris Gantry (second from left) listen to one of Shel Silverstein's most assuredly rousing performances.

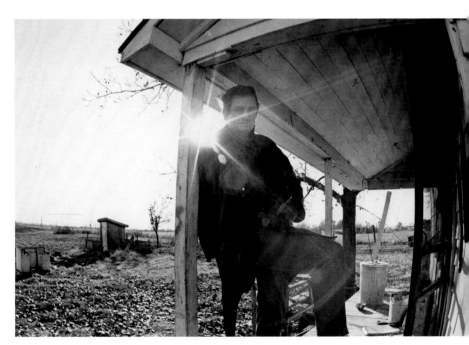

My father on the front porch of the house he grew up in, in Dyess, Arkansas.

me of Dad's best photographs are of people, nature, and animals. This is a young me playing with a frog in the
ont yard at Cinnamon Hill, Jamacia.

My Dad and me with my grandfather, Ezra "Pop" Carter. My son, Jack Ezra, carries on his namesake.

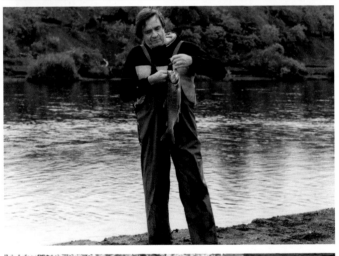

Dad with a nice catch on the banks of a wilderness river in Alaska.

Family and friends, including my grandfather, Ray (seated, in the red plaid), and uncle, Roy (seated, in the black shirt), on a hunting trip to Kingsland, Arkansas, Dad's birthplace, in 1976. Dad's first cousin, Mark Rivers (far right), still lives there and hunts the same land.

y Dad and I heading to the Grammy Living Legends Awards Show in New York City in 1991. I'm pretty sure the
nousine behind us is the same one I mention in Chapter One. We used the same driver and car for years.

y son, Joseph, Dad, Rosanne, and my mother relax and play Carter Family music on the front porch of the Carter
mily home in Hiltons, Virginia.

My parent's last portrait as a couple.

When my mother passed, a portion of my father went with her—they were closer and more in love than ever before in their later years. But Dad never lost sight of what he believed in, never lost his passion. I believe that now their love is only that much greater.

came to Hendersonville to make music with Dad. I was there for almost all of these sessions and learned two things: when to keep my mouth shut and when to chime in with an opinion, though during the early recordings, I was more vocal than I needed to be. Rick is wonderful in the studio. He seems to know how to direct the session without being imposing—how to help the process along without complicating things. I learned a great deal from Rick in those sessions.

My wife, Laura Cash (Laura Weber at the time), took part in some of those early recordings at the cabin. Dad loved her fiddle playing. She brought him a good few songs, including "I'm Free from the Chain Gang Now" and "The Evening Train." Laura remembers the first day she went into the studio with Dad. I was engineering. A friend and wonderful old-time guitar player named Larry Perkins (no relation to Luther Perkins, Dad's longtime guitar player), Laura, Dad, and I were the only ones there that day.

"The energy that day was intense," said Laura. "It was intimate and intimidating at the same time. It was so quiet in that room. There were candles lit and everything was peaceful, but I was nervous and in awe. It was the first time I'd ever been around him in that type of environment."

We recorded a version of "Wayfaring Stranger" that day, another of Laura's suggestions. Laura and Larry accompanied Dad as he sang and played guitar.

"At first," said Laura, "I was playing lines with more notes. He said, 'Play longer lines and fewer notes.' The next pass through he turned to me and said, 'How does it feel to play on a Grammy Award–winning album?' That was when I knew I had done something right. It felt like we were the only people on the face of the earth." The album did, in fact, go on to win a Grammy, just as Dad had predicted.

These sessions at the cabin went on for the rest of Dad's life. Some of the recordings for the remaining American albums were done at Rick's studio in California, but a great deal were recorded at what became known as Cash Cabin Studio. There were many great musicians who took part in these sessions, such as Randy Scruggs, Marty Stuart, Pat McLaughlin, Benmont Tench, Smokey Hormel, and Mike Campbell, to name a few. The recordings at the cabin carried on even when Rick wasn't there. David Ferguson, my brother-in-law Jimmy Tittle, and I facilitated the production as best we could.

Rick deserves a lot of credit for his work with Dad, but every producer who has worked with my father has admitted that Johnny Cash was not really produced—you just stood back and tried to capture what happened. Dad always had a vision for his projects, bringing his own songs and other favorites to the table. He had a unique ability to determine whether a song could work for him. And he was never wrong about it. When Rick brought Dad "Turn, Turn, Turn," by the Byrds, my father knew very well it was a wonderful song but decided quickly he would not record it. He said it was just not right for him. Alternatively, when Rick brought Dad "Hurt," he immediately knew it was a good choice. He took these songs, including "Personal Jesus," "Solitary Man," "Desperado," and the raucous "Rusty Cage" and made them his own. I brought my father a few good songs, though he passed on more than he recorded. But when I played him Sting's "I Hung

Even when my father was seriously ill, he never gave up dreaming and not once lost his inspiration; if anything, he redoubled his efforts.

My Head" and Bruce Springsteen's "Further On (Up the Road)," he immediately knew they would work for him.

There were many studio days that I remember well. On one occasion we were recording for *American IV* in Los Angeles at Rick's home studio, the Akademie Mathematique of Philosophical Sound Research. That week was very successful. Dad had already cut "Desperado," "Bridge Over Troubled Water," and some others that would later become a part of the final CD. Joe Strummer of the Clash had been hanging out all week, and we began that day working with Joe. (Not long after this, Joe died of cancer.) Rick had suggested "One Love" by Bob Marley, but though Dad loved the song, he had determined it was not for him. Looking through the Marley repertoire, we rediscovered "Redemption Song." Smokey Hormel sang the tracking vocal while a song was recorded. We continued this process the whole week, especially when Dad wasn't completely familiar with the song. We would find the right key for him and then someone would sing the live tracking vocal while Dad sat back and listened to the recording taking place, oftentimes offering input and direction. By the time we were through, Dad usually felt up to the task and would go in and sing the song a few times through—and generally did not need to sing it again.

After a particularly moving recording of the Marley song (which may be heard on the American Recordings' *Unearthed* box set), we decided to try the recording of "Hurt." I knew the song by heart, having been a fan of Nine Inch Nails for years. I sang it live with the band that day, and the experience will never leave me. I had the chance to be a part of the formulation of this recording with Smokey, Benmont, and Mike Campbell. What these musicians did was perfect for my father. It was like watching magic take place. Immediately after we finished tracking the song, Dad went in and sang it.

That week we wrapped up *American IV* and went home, but Dad would not take a break. Within a few days, we were back in the studio working on *American V*.

During this recording process, Dad's health typically was not good. He was losing his sight, and his diabetes was sapping his strength. Dad probably had diabetes for many years and left it untreated. It was only the last year of his life that he accepted the disease and took steps toward treatment.

All this time, through these struggles, sicknesses, and triumphs, my parents' love for each other gave them both a lot of strength. They had ceased fighting altogether and never bickered in the least. They had come to accept each other unconditionally, and it showed in their everyday life. They were always affectionate and loving to each other. Somehow their love had not only endured but grown. My mother and father were each other's best friends.

I don't believe anyone, with the exception of my mother and possibly her doctor, knew the extent of her heart trouble. But my mother expressed a great peace in what seemed a conscious knowledge of her approaching end. I remember very clearly the last day I spoke to her in May 2003. She was weak although smiling, going through her jewelry, picking out pieces to give away to her daughters and friends. She had a great sadness in her eyes that day, and yet along with the sadness was peace. She had come to terms with her life and was happy with it. I think my father also sensed Mom's life was winding down. Perhaps their joint realization had brought them closer together.

The next day Mom went to the hospital with chest pains, weakness, and difficulty breathing. Within a week, she was dead.

My father had lost his best friend, his other half. He was heartbroken. However, in the face of this greatest of life's pains, one he had not encountered with such intensity since losing his brother Jack, he did not stop. He kept recording. The first session Dad did after the funeral was a project I was producing as a tribute to the Carter Family, called *The Unbroken Circle*. The first song he recorded was a beautiful one called "I Found You Among the Roses"—as of now unreleased. Rick came for the sessions a few days later, during which we recorded "God's Gonna Cut You Down" and "Ain't No Grave Gonna Hold My Body Down."

It was as if in the grip of such great pain, all Dad could do was sing and find solace in his music. By the summer he was functionally blind. All his books sat on his shelf unread. This was another sadness. He could no longer pursue his lifelong passion for reading; even his Bible sat gathering dust on his desk. He was consumed by depression, to be sure, but he did not stop. To me this was a demonstration of the greatest courage. What greater work can there be than that which is done during such a trying time? Does this not define a person as even greater than the work done in the prime of life? What my father was made of was quite apparent during these last months of his life.

When it was announced that the video for the song "Hurt" was up for the Best Cinematography Award on the MTV Video Music Awards show, Dad refused to hear that he could not go. He was determined. He bought his ticket and we all planned to attend. But when the date approached, he fell ill and was forced to go into the hospital to deal with another bout of pneumonia. It was not his spirit that gave up in the end, but his body. If not for his physical illnesses, he would have carried on. Many say that my father died of a broken heart. I do not believe this is true. I believe he died with a broken heart, but it did not kill him.

After he got out of the hospital that time and came home, we were back in the studio. We had put on an addition to the cabin, and Dad was excited to use his new recording room. He cut his unforgettable "Like the 309," laughing in the face of illness right to the end.

I remember vividly the day my father was taken to the hospital for the last time. I had rushed over to the house from the cabin when I got the call he was very ill. I arrived just as the ambulance was about to pull out. I approached Dad, who had an oxygen mask over his face.

"I love you, Dad," I said. "You're gonna be just fine."

He did not respond, but I will never forget the look in his eyes. It was a look that said "not this time." I had seen this same look in my mother's eyes just a few months before.

That same night, my sisters Rosanne, Kathy, and I gathered around his bed and Dad passed out of this world and into the next. I believe his greatest emotion as he left this world was overwhelming excitement to see my mother's face again.

So who was this man, this enigma? Who was he beneath the rugged exterior? How could he make us so easily believe he was either a devil or an angel, and sit beside the president one day and a farmer the next (and often did), equally at ease beside either one? How did he become this man, so deep and mysterious, yet so open and accessible, all at the same time?

Dad had a great love of nature and the outdoors, where he sometimes sought solitude. He spent long periods of time throughout his life alone. I believe it was his isolation, in part, that made us want to be closer to him, to comfort him and be comforted by him.

My father was continuously searching. He searched so far and long, carrying his loved ones with him on his quests. And we looked up to him, seeking his wisdom and guidance, though at times he admittedly could offer neither. And throughout his restless struggles, his loss and pain, if he had been asked "What are you looking for?" surely he would have answered with resounding truthfulness that he had found his treasure long, long before: his salvation from God. And yet he was never full.

Dad's influence on our musical culture is unequaled. His music can be heard in every corner of the planet. It is with honesty and an almost childlike self-effacement that he found a way into the public's heart, without even seeming to try.

I encounter him somewhere every day. I see him on the television and on the Internet, and I hear him on the radio. His life story has been immortalized on film, radio, and television. There are various documentaries, which air often. New fans are introduced to his life and music regularly through the film *Walk the Line*, which won many awards, including two Golden Globes plus an Oscar for Reese Witherspoon's portrayal of my mother.

When Larry King asked my father on his show what he would most like to be remembered for, Dad's initial and heartfelt response was that he would like to be remembered as a good father. In this, his legacy is safe. All my siblings and I remember him that way. There were, of course, times when he fell short, as we all do. But in the final analysis, the scales tip heavily in his favor, and the wounds have healed and been forgiven.

Every day, when people hear the steady boom-chicka-boom over a speaker in a public place and are introduced to the music of Johnny Cash, many are intrigued enough to learn more about his music. Upon investigation, those new fans find there is a lot of depth to the music and the man. It's something that continually impresses everyone who has known him. As we all look deeper, we may feel confused and intrigued. Then as we peel away the final layers and peek into the heart of all that may be known about the man, we discover his faith, his love for God, his passion for what is right, and his ultimate strength. God stood with him through it all. Dad was a tool for God's work. All the darkness and toughness amount to one thing: a lure to reel us in for a closer look so that when we see behind the illusion, we find a simple, kind man who had faith in God.

CHAPTER TEN

REFLECTIONS FROM FAMILY & FRIENDS

ne of my father's favorite Scriptures was Galatians 5:22–23: "But the fruit of the Spirit is love, joy, peace, forbearance, kindness, goodness, faithfulness, gentleness, and self-control. Against such things there is no law." These qualities were characteristic of the friendship and love Dad gave to the people in his life. And though many of his best friends happened to be wealthy or celebrities, he never chose them based on their status.

One of my father's best friends in the world was a good man from Hickman County, Tennessee, named Luther Fleaner. Luther is retired now, though for years he worked at the Ford glass plant in Nashville and looked after Dad's farm in Bon Aqua, Tennessee. Luther and Dad spent a great deal of time together. When I was young, Luther would take Dad and me coon hunting, which to those who do not know, is the process of chasing howling coon-hounds through the darkened woods with flashlights and guns. That is to say, we spent a lot of time sitting around a campfire and chewing tobacco. When the dogs began to "bay," meaning their howls became stationary, it was a sign they had run an ani-mal up a tree—usually a possum. These were good, simple times when my father, Luther, and I really enjoyed ourselves. Dad loved Luther because they related at the level of the heart.

Some of Dad's dearest friends have passed away, including Dr. Nat Winston, Waylon Jennings, and John Rollins, but there are still a good few around. He is remembered fondly by so many—family members, dear friends, colleagues in the music industry, and those who simply love his music. On the following pages are a few reflections from some who were dear to my father, loved him throughout his life, and cherish their memories of the time they spent with him. He meant many different things to the people who contributed to this chapter, but they all loved him dearly.

LAURA CASH

My wife, Laura, is a spiritual, strong-natured, talented, and family-centered woman. When my mother and father met her, they were immediately attracted to her and saw her for just what she was: the real deal. But most important, my parents sensed that she would be a wonderful, loving, and caring mother to our children. Laura worked with Dad a few times in the studio, but she knew him mostly as our children's grandfather, which he took the utmost joy in always. —JCC

John Cash was a fantastic grandpa. He was gentle, patient, loving, and involved in his grandkids' lives. It was obvious that they brought him a great deal of joy.

There was a thing he did with the babies: He would tightly cradle them up against his chest and sing to them in his lowest voice, "Boom-bobba-boom-bobba-boom-ba-boom-baboom" over and over to a rockabilly-type rhythm. The vibration from his chest could be felt across the room. It would entrance the babe in his arms.

When our daughter, Anna Maybelle, was just over a year old, we were up in Virginia at the Carter family home, recording June's *Wildwood Flower* album. Anna Maybelle (AnnaBelle, as she likes to be called) was sitting on her grandpa's lap at supper, picking food off his plate. He always had a separate plate of sliced tomatoes and raw onions. She started eating those raw onions, and he just beamed with pride. "She's a Cash!" he said. I began to worry that the onions would make her sick, mixed with the bottle she just had. I said, "John, she's eating a lot of those onions, you may want to . . . " Before I could finish, he said, "Leave her alone, Mom," and offered her another piece. To this day raw onion is one of her favorite foods.

After June died, when AnnaBelle was two, we would take her to visit John often. She would make a beeline for his room, where she knew he would be. Before we could even get there ourselves, she was up in his lap, eating out of his stash of sugar-free milk chocolate. He would sit so patiently with her, as she would feed him little tiny champagne grapes, one at a time, for what seemed like hours. He would always perk up when he saw her.

John had an infectious youthful spirit, which really came alive when his grandchildren were around. I see John in the spirit of all of our children. Joseph spent a lot of time with him as a young child, and AnnaBelle as well. Jack, the namesake of John's adored brother, never got to meet his grandpa, but he may resemble his grandfather the most—he's mischievous, generous, and loving. His birthday is February 27, the day after his grandfather's birthday.

—LAURA

JOANNE CASH YATES

Joanne Cash Yates is my father's younger sister. She grew up, like all the Cash children, picking cotton in Dyess, Arkansas. Today, she is a pastor and spiritual advisor living in Hendersonville, Tennessee. Her husband, Harry Yates, is also a pastor. —JCC

Johnny was six years older than me, but being raised in cotton country, age didn't matter; we all worked side by side every day. Johnny (JR to me) was just my brother. We did everything together, all of us. We worked, played, went to church, but most of all, I remember the singing. We sang in the cotton fields, in church, and around Mama's old upright piano every night, as Mama played. We listened to the radio as much as possible, until Daddy told us to turn it off to save the battery! JR was *always* writing songs.

After Jack died, we became closer than ever before. JR was always gentle, and he never said an unkind word to me that I can remember. He was always there for me. JR said to me when I was ten or twelve, "Try to always do things right." He also said Jesus loved me, and then he said, "I love you, too." Another time he told me, "Sing with all your heart and as long as you can. You can do anything as long as you let Jesus guide you," and then he looked at me with his magical grin and gave me a hug. In my life now, I miss him so very much, but the memory of the many things he told me are with me daily, and I will treasure these gifts for the rest of my life.

—JOANNE

CINDY CASH PANETTA

Cindy Cash is my sister, Dad's third daughter. Right now she lives in Ventura, California, but is considering moving back to Hendersonville. —JCC

I was nine years old when my mother and father divorced. Dad moved to Nashville and Mom remained in Ventura. I spent the next nine years yearning for my dad. Although I was close with my mother, my heart ached, and I had an ardent desire to know my father better, to be close to him.

In 1977, when I was eighteen and newly divorced with a baby girl, I received a call from Dad urging me to move to Tennessee. I spent the next twenty-three years in Hendersonville, Tennessee, and Dad and I became very close. I was the epitome of a daddy's girl and loved it. He became the dad I had missed through those years, my confidant and the person I depended on for all of life's lessons.

In 1990, Dad and I were in a counseling session together. Long story but short answer. The therapist had asked us to sit facing one another, knees to knees. She asked Dad to name the one thing he appreciated most about me. His answer spoke volumes to me and showed me a side of Dad that I remained fiercely protective of. His response was, "I've never had to doubt for a second that Cindy truly loves me."

I remember little else of that day.

—CINDY

TOMMY CASH

Tommy Cash is my father's younger brother. Tommy is a successful performer and musician in his own right. As children growing up in Dyess, Arkansas, Tommy and Dad were close, though separated by eight years. Dad always referred lovingly to Tommy as his kid brother. —JCC

John told me, "Always follow your dreams. Don't let anything stand in your way." He also advised me, "Don't let people who ask you constantly, 'Are you really Johnny's brother?' bother you to the point to where it affects your goals." So I tell people who ask, "I knew Johnny like a brother." He was big brother to me long before he was Johnny Cash.

—TOMMY

ROSANNE CASH

I have looked up to my sister Rosanne my entire life. She is strong and has been guided by her sense of morality and independent spirit throughout her life. Her music is her own and her artistry, unequaled. From the time I was young, I recall her laughter filling the house. I cherish her now as my oldest sibling and respect her to the utmost. When my mother passed, Rosanne gave up her life for at least a month and moved in with Dad to stay close. She was there for him during that time, supporting him and selflessly giving of her heart. For this, as our father was, I will always be grateful. —JCC

When I was nineteen years old, I was lying on my bed reading a book, and my dad walked into the room. "What are you reading?" he asked. I showed him the cover. "It's a book on astrology," I said. I waited for a sign of disapproval, but he just nodded. I pushed it a bit: "You don't believe in this, do you?" I asked. "No," he said, "but I think you should find out everything you can about it." His attitude was so generous and that sentence was so loving and spontaneous, that I was instantly filled with love and a giddy sense of liberation.

That was my dad in a nutshell, and that was his style of parenting. He treated people with respect; he encouraged curiosity; he reveled in freedom, and wanted others to do the same. And he had a basic belief that everyone had a right and an obligation to examine their own ideas, beliefs, principles, and opinions.

He didn't judge, and he thought the world could accommodate a lot of very different people. It was the best lesson in parenting I could possibly receive and a graceful example of how to treat everyone.

I've never forgotten it, and today I remind myself to ask my children for their opinions, to listen to their crazy ideas, even to watch them reject what I hold dear, without judgment, so that they might find out who they are, what they believe, and what they love. That little exchange between Dad and me gave me confidence and a feeling that I could be self-determined and that my curiosity was welcome, even essential. I don't think he ever knew how important that moment was to me. I filed it away in a corner of myself, and I let it grow and change me until it was so much a part of the fabric of my own psyche that it seemed unnecessary and redundant to put words to it. But today, without my dad in this wide world, about which he was so curious, and in which he took up so much space with such grace, I wish I had told him how grateful I was for a single sentence he said to me when I was a teenager, when he was just being himself, when he was curious about what I was doing with my mind, when he wanted me to find out everything I could about everything.

—ROSANNE

THE ROLLINS FAMILY

John and Michele Rollins were longtime friends of my parents. We spent a great deal of time in Jamaica with the Rollins family growing up. Their children, Michael, Monique, Mark, and Michele, and John's older son, Ted, were all my parents' godchildren. Unlike the many people in my parents' lives who tugged at them and demanded things of them, the Rollins family spent time with my parents simply because they enjoyed their company. —JCC

MICHELE ROLLINS

Johnny Cash, the man, the singer, the composer, the legend: I took those things for granted when I met him in 1976 backstage at Wolf Trap, in Virginia.

During a financial downturn for my husband, John Rollins, Johnny bought Cinnamon Hill Great House as a show of support, but more importantly, as a show of friendship. As is so often the case, gestures from the heart bring much happiness. Cinnamon Hill became a resting place, a place of solace and rejuvenation, and a place of joy and music where the private Johnny Cash enjoyed time with his soul mate, June, and spent time reading about the things that meant so much to him: history, geography, philosophy, and so much more.

I was always struck by the generosity of spirit demonstrated by Johnny and June, very uncommon to stars of their caliber. There were no young talents they didn't support by allowing them to appear on their live show. Never mind that they allowed my guitarist son Ted, flute-playing son Michael, and daughter Monique, a singer, to be in the show repeatedly. After all, they were godparents to all of our children. But the list of those very talented stars who got their start with Johnny and June is well known; some became legends in their own right.

When John Rollins died in 2000, there was a hole in my heart I thought would never heal. And when Johnny and June died so soon after in 2003, I wondered if my heart could ever fill with joy again. But when I look around and see my children and grand-children, so full of the love my John and Johnny and June gave them, my broken heart is restored.

—MICHELE

MICHAEL ROLLINS

Writing this is difficult for me because it means acknowledging he is gone. The echoes of his voice are still around me. He was con-sistently open and honest, as much as anyone I have ever known. I felt like I could ask him anything. Thinking of him reminds me that imperfection can be so much more refreshing and interesting. He never claimed to be a saint, and he helps me see, to this day, that a single mistake is not the end of the world but the basis of who you become. I knew of many of the mistakes he had made, of his addic-tion. His life was an open book to me—a book that I wish I had inquired more deeply into. And now the more I think of him, the more I write, the closer I feel to him. I guess this is how love works.

—MICHAEL

TED ROLLINS

One of the most important things that JR said to me was after my father died. In his low, calm voice he said rather matter-of-factly, "Ted, you know when a parent dies that means a couple of things; you take on all of their good qualities, and you have a special angel up in heaven to watch out over you." I have carried those words with me since that day.

When I was much younger (and even more impressionable), we were walking somewhere one day, and part of the walk was through a restricted area. I said to him, "John, you know we aren't supposed to be going through here." And he replied, "If you just throw your shoulders back, walk fast, and act like you are supposed to be here, no one will ever bother you."

John to me was freedom from the ordinary, freedom from the bonds of normalcy. He taught me the importance and joy found in the little things, like frying ham in the morning or a good fire—or blowing things up. He was a great teacher and a very patient one at that. I always felt he understood me and that he had a deep insight into all the craziness in my life—good and bad.

—TED

KRIS & LISA KRISTOFFERSON

Kris Kristofferson was one of my father's closest friends, truly more like a brother. When Kris first met Dad, my father knew immediately he was something special, although at the time he was a janitor at a recording studio. My father saw Kris's vision and loved him for his spirit and his passion. Dad perceived in Kris a man who was not afraid to stand up for what he believed in, and in this they were very much alike. Kris and my father worked together on many occasions. In the mid-1980s they collaborated with Waylon Jennings and Willie Nelson as the Highwaymen. But it was as friends that Dad and Kris's relationship was strongest. —JCC

KRIS KRISTOFFERSON

Of the many blessings in my life, perhaps the greatest—aside from my family—is that so many of my heroes have become my close friends, beautifully enriching my time on the planet. I'm especially grateful to Johnny Cash for helping me become who I want to be.

The exhilarating electricity of his handshake backstage at the Grand Ole Opry put the final nail in the coffin of my military career. And his subsequent encouragement of my songwriting during my years as a janitor at the recording studio (he carried the lyrics to one of my songs in his wallet) were all I needed. Four years later, his recording of "Sunday Morning Coming Down," which I had written, won the Country Music Association's Song of the Year. And even before that, the door was always open at his house on the lake to me and a few of my songwriter friends. When I was working on the offshore oil rigs in the Gulf, he made me famous in the oil fields when he called to tell me Luther Perkins, John's guitarist from 1955 through 1968, had died. Later, he put me onstage with him at the Newport Folk Festival (against their wishes), and I never had to work a day job again. The next thing I knew, I was standing next to him onstage performing all over the world with the Highwaymen.

The only advice I can remember him giving me was at Newport, when he said, "Try to sing louder. I can barely hear you in the room." It was the honesty and the power of his performance that showed me what to aim for. Aside from my wife and kids, he's the greatest blessing in my life.

—KRIS

Lisa Kristofferson was a close friend to my parents for many years and spent a great deal of time with my mother and father. Her children knew my parents as an aunt and uncle, and Mom and Dad were also the godparents of the Kristoffersons' son, Johnny. Lisa is one of the strongest people I know, tough and loving. Like my mother, she considers family closeness the most important thing in life. When my mother passed away and I was in my worst pain, Lisa was there beside me, undaunted, comforting, and giving. I will always cherish her for that. —JCC

LISA KRISTOFFERSON

I was two months pregnant with our second son, Jody, when Kris and I were invited to Montreaux, Switzerland, to participate in The Johnny Cash Christmas Special, along with Willie and Connie

Nelson and Waylon and Jessi Jennings. It was here that I was first introduced to the tradition of the songwriter's circle. Willie, Waylon, John, and Kris took turns with June and Jessi filling in any harmony gaps. I was moved to tears many times, and June asked me to chime in whenever I wanted. I made a joke about how I am the one person in my family who was told that I shouldn't sing, not even in the shower. Johnny looked right through me and said, "That may be true, but we performers hear ourselves through your eyes and we need that." He gave me a purpose: I could listen with awe and respect, and that's what I did for the next fifteen years of my life as I toured with the Highwaymen.

There are so many times during those years that John directed us back to what was real and what was important. Maybe because he had the wisdom as the eldest of the Highwaymen, but also because what he said always rang true, like the voice of God. He always remembered to say "I love you" and always said your name afterward: "I love you, Lisa." But it wasn't just that—he seemed always to mean it, too.

Toward the end of his life, on one of his reentries into the hospital, I had each of our kids write a get-well letter to him. He called when he received them and said that he had never received letters that meant more to him—not from presidents or kings. Children were his absolute joy. After June's funeral, I saw him swarmed by his grandchildren and smiled. Despite his failing health and immeasurable grief, the kids were there to keep him strong.

—LISA

LOU ROBIN

Lou Robin was Dad's manager for most of their respective careers. He continues to manage the Cash estate and protect my father's legacy. All those years I traveled with my father on the road show playing guitar and singing my part, Lou was there on every tour. He is one of the toughest men I know—determined and sharp, always looking out for Dad's best interests, and now, looking after his legacy. For many years Dad did not even have a contract with Lou, just a handshake agreement. —JCC

My company, Artists Consultants Productions, Inc., began promoting Johnny Cash concerts in 1969 and then progressed to the management position in 1973.

My relationship with John gave me the greatest respect for his genius as a composer, artist, and poet. His instinct when making decisions about his music and other business matters was uncanny. John was always honorable in his dealings. Despite his shortcomings, John was concerned about his fellow man. He was also that rare entertainer who could thrill audiences throughout the world the moment he took the stage.

Something John said to me once while we were traveling through Germany made a big impression, giving me a glimpse of a different side of the man: "Hey Lou! We need to cancel the shows tonight and tomorrow. John Carter (then age four or five) wants to go see some castles."

My life was profoundly affected by the wisdom gained from the many years I spent with John on and off the road. Having known him, it is fascinating to see his influence on young and old alike through his music and writings. I'm sure this will continue to be so for generations to come.

—LOU

JACK SHAW

Rev. Jack Shaw was a friend and confidant for many years, traveling on Dad's road show and offering spiritual support and guidance. During the time Jack was on the road with us, we had a devotional before each show. We would all hold hands in a quiet corner of the backstage area (which was not always easy to find) and pray. —JCC

In 1993 John and I were in Branson, Missouri, talking backstage one evening. Just before the show started, he said, "Call me every day, Jack." "Every day?" I asked. "Every day. Around ten in the morning or seven in the evening." It was the most important thing he'd ever said to me.

For many years that followed, I did exactly that. Whether we were at home or on the road, on different floors in a hotel, or on opposite sides of the world, I would call him every day. Those calls were so precious. We'd discuss a variety of subjects as good friends do: problems, concerns, family, health, challenges—so many things. But ultimately, no matter the subject, we would end up discussing something spiritual, usually faith in the midst of adversity. We would talk about the Bible and what God's Word might have to say to us about heaven, loved ones who had passed away, or a favorite or particular verse.

John was compassionate to all and especially those down and out. He was strong in character (although a bit shy), fully committed to what he believed in, and an extremely bright and gifted individual. Often, when facing life's problematic challenges and/ or difficulties, I ask myself, "What would John do; how would he conduct himself in this situation?" And, truly, doing so usually brings a perspective into focus that had not been there before.

John often said, "One of these days I'm going to set down and talk to Paul." One day I shall do likewise, but I must admit I am most excited about someday once again sitting down and talking to John.

—JACK

Dad and his spiritual advisor, Jack Shaw, onstage in Branson, Missouri.

JACK CLEMENT

Jack Clement was one of my father's best friends, confidants, and a producer of his music for many years. They were just plain silly together. Jack and Dad first met in Memphis in the mid-1950s, while Jack was the engineer at Sun Records. —JCC

I am very happy and proud that I got to spend a lot of time with Johnny Cash in a lot of places: Memphis, Nashville, New York City, Hawaii, Jamaica, Australia, Ireland, Scotland, England, Germany, and several other spots. Working with John was always fun, inspiring, and musical. I miss him every day.

—JACK

TOP | *Dad and Jack Clement lean out of Jack's office window. They were forever joking around.*
BOTTOM | *Norman Blake (right), Dad, and me on the front porch of the Cash Cabin Studio in Hendersonville, Tennessee.*

145

MY FRIEND, THE FAMOUS PERSON
by Jack H. Clement

———————————•———————————

My friend, the famous person, is a barrel full of fun,
a rather shy guy, a very nice guy,
in spite of all he's done.
He's been around, this friend of mine,
ten times ten and then again.
Down the river 'round the world
and up the creek times ten.

For springing back brings secret laughter
and toughens up the chinny-chin
and lets the player fall down harder
just to get to bat again.
To really know a fellow person takes a while, you know;
it's seldom easy but easily worth it
just to find a kindred soul.
A kindred soul will pass the test or flunk it just for spite;
just to enjoy being a human,
so let him do it—it's his right.

Scold him quickly if he needs it
and never be a yes-ing man;
tell him no when no's the answer
or a lie he'll love and understand.

A kindred soul comes back around
and never really leaves;
though some time may pass
while he seems like an ass,
he'll show up in one of your dreams.

My friend, the famous person,
is a pal you might know, too,
for he has a lot of friends
and that's what makes him true.
A true friend will realize
there's more to the truth
than absence of lies.
It takes a good man to take success
and not misplace his soul
while bumbling through the facts of life
and too much rock and roll.
He's a hero still drifting upward,
ever rising 'cross the land,
ever learning, ever earning
my attention span.

ABOUT THE AUTHOR

John Carter Cash has been surrounded by music his whole life, writing songs and staying active in the creative process. He is the only son of John R. Cash and June Carter Cash. He preserves the family legacy and is caretaker to the heritage of his musical ancestors.

A successful music producer, John Carter has been a producer on five Grammy Award–winning albums, including his mother June Carter Cash's *Press On* (1999), and has worked with Rick Rubin as Associate Producer on his father's *American III: Solitary Man* and *American IV: The Man Comes Around*, the latter receiving three Country Music Association awards. He owns and operates the Cash Cabin Studio and Cash Productions, LLC, near Nashville, Tennessee.

John Carter is the author of *Anchored in Love: An Intimate Portrait of June Carter Cash*, a biography of his mother, as well as several children's books.

Cash lives with his wife, Laura, and their three children in Hendersonville, Tennessee.

www.johncartercash.com

AUTHOR'S ACKNOWLEDGMENTS

Acknowledgments are due to those who were a part of the making of this book. First, I offer thanks to God for being my strength. Thanks to my editor, Kate Etue, for sticking with this and having faith. I am grateful to Jake Gerli and everyone at Insight Editions for seeing the possibilities for this book and helping to make it a reality. Thanks to Deborah Kops for the painstaking copyediting and to Michel Vrána for the wondrous design work.

Great thanks to Lou Robin, who still maintains and manages the Johnny Cash estate. Lou is the ultimate watchdog and stays true to my father's morals and goals, the same now as when the man was alive. He was an important sounding board for me throughout the process of putting this book together.

Special thanks to those who contributed: Billy Graham, Rosanne Cash, Lisa and Kris Kristofferson, Cindy Cash Panetta, Tommy Cash, Joanne Cash Yates, Michael and Michele Rollins, Ted Rollins, Jack Shaw, and "Cowboy" Jack Clement. Thanks to Allison McCoury and Lauren Moore for the invaluable organizational skills and patience, and to Kyle Gregory, Tom and Geri Moore, and Lisa Trice. Thanks to Maury Scobee, Marty Stuart, Chance Martin, Daniel Coston, Alan Messer, Amelia Davis, and Annie Leibovitz.

And my utmost gratitude to my wife, Laura Cash, who stuck with me through the writing and is always there, through it all.

And to Mark Stielper, who puts the utmost care and love into anything he does. Thanks for the invaluable help and for watching my back.

Originally published in deluxe hardcover edition by Insight Editions,
San Rafael, CA, in 2011.

INSIGHT
EDITIONS

PO Box 3088
San Rafael, CA 94912
www.insighteditions.com

Library of Congress Cataloging-in-Publication Data available.

ISBN: 978-1-60887-479-8

 ROOTS of PEACE   REPLANTED PAPER

Insight Editions, in association with Roots of Peace, will plant two trees
for each tree used in the manufacturing of this book. Roots of Peace is an
internationally renowned humanitarian organization dedicated to eradicat-
ing land mines worldwide and converting war-torn lands into productive
farms and wildlife habitats. Together, we will plant two million fruit and nut
trees in Afghanistan and provide farmers there with the skills and support
necessary for sustainable land use.

Manufactured in China by Insight Editions

10 9 8 7 6 5 4 3 2 1

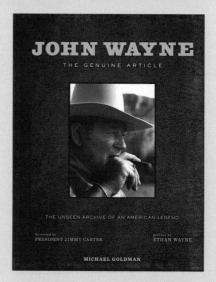